NEW
AVENGERS
BREAKOUT

W9-AVN-654

MARVEL

A NOVEL OF THE MARVEL UNIVERSE

NEW AVENGERS

BREAKOUT

BASED ON THE COMIC SERIES BY BRIAN MICHAEL BENDIS AND DAVID FINCH

ALISA KWITNEY

NEW AVENGERS: BREAKOUT. Published by MARVEL WORLDWIDE, INC., a subsidiary of MARVEL ENTERTAINMENT, LLC. OFFICE OF PUBLICATION: 135 West 50th Street, New York, NY, 10020. Copyright © 2013 Marvel Characters, Inc. All rights reserved.

ISBN# 978-0-7851-6517-0.

Printed in the U.S.A.

ALAN FINE, EVP - Office of the President, Marvel Worldwide, Inc. and EVP & CMO Marvel Characters B.V.; DAN BUCKLEY, Publisher & President - Print, Animation & Digital Divisions; JOE QUESADA, Chief Creative Officer; TOM BREVOORT, SVP of Publishing; DAVID BOGART, SVP of Operations & Procurement, Publishing; C.B. CEBULSKI, SVP of Creator & Content Development; DAVID GABRIEL, SVP of Print & Digital Publishing Sales; JIM O'KEEFE, VP of Operations & Logistics; DAN CARR, Executive Director of Publishing Technology; SUSAN CRESPI, Editorial Operations Manager; ALEX MORALES, Publishing Operations Manager; STAN LEE, Chairman Emeritus. For information regarding advertising in Marvel Comics or on Marvel.com, please contact Niza Disla, Director of Marvel Partnerships, at ndisla@marvel.com. For Marvel subscription inquiries, please call 800-217-9158. **Manufactured between 8/16/13 and 9/8/13 by SHERIDAN BOOKS, INC., CHELSEA, MI, USA.**

First printing 2013

10 9 8 7 6 5 4 3 2 1

Front Cover Art by David Finch and Danny Miki

Back Cover Art by Daniel Acuña

Interior art by David Finch, Mark Bagley, and Danny Miki

Stuart Moore, Editor

Design by Spring Hoteling

Senior Editor, Special Projects: Jeff Youngquist

SVP of Print & Digital Publishing Sales: David Gabriel

Editor in Chief: Axel Alonso

Chief Creative Officer: Joe Quesada

Publisher: Dan Buckley

Executive Producer: Alan Fine

TO: MATTHEW AND ELINOR

Thanks to Ray Teetsel for martial arts and archery advice, retired Navy Seal Karl Swepston and his wife, A.E. for some special ops pointers and Elena Sherman for Russian phrases. Jeff, thank you for sending me reference on a dime when needed, and, Stuart, I can't tell you how much I appreciate your calm voice leading me out of the maze of dark corridors. Any mistakes are entirely my own fault.

And last but not least, thanks to Brian Bendis, for letting me play in the clubhouse he built.

NEW AVENGERS

BREAKOUT

A NOVEL OF THE
MARVEL UNIVERSE

ONE

THERE was something about the redhead that caught Clint Barton's attention. It wasn't her wickedly pretty face or her exceptional rear view, although those were certainly worth noticing. No, it was something subtly discordant, something that made Clint think Red didn't belong up here in the command center of the Strategic Homeland Intervention Enforcement and Logistics Division.

Clint furrowed his brow. He might only have a level-six clearance, but as he observed the shapely interloper move with unhurried ease through a room bristling with S.H.I.E.L.D. agents, he didn't see anyone else clocking her progress across the bridge. There were more than a few guys watching her, but they didn't look like they had surveillance on their minds. Leaning back in his chair, Clint tried to figure out what it was about Red that didn't fit. Unlike a lot of the glorified clerks in this room, he hadn't gotten a bunch of degrees from some Ivy League institution, but what he did have was a circus brat's skill in picking out the rubes from the roustabouts. At first glance, Red appeared to be dressed in a figure-hugging black jumpsuit identical to the ones worn by S.H.I.E.L.D. pilots and combat-trained operatives. On closer inspection, Clint noticed that her uniform had no insignia on the arm—and the weapon hanging from the holster on her slim hips didn't have the shiny, streamlined look of something concocted by Stark Enterprises.

So not a rube, but not a member of this particular traveling show, either.

"Clint? You about finished with that report?" Jessica Drew glanced at him, still managing to tap away at her computer. Like him, Jessica was a field agent, but she had probably filed three reports in the time it had taken him to type his Social Security number. She was the only agent who never asked him about his criminal record, so he returned the favor by never bringing up the fact that she used to have super-powers. For Clint, being a S.H.I.E.L.D. agent was a giant step up in life. For the former Spider-Woman, he figured, it was something else entirely.

"If you're having trouble with the spreadsheet, I can help you," she offered.

"Nah, I'll figure it out." Clint had spent his school years perfecting his acrobatic and archery skills, so there were some pretty big gaps in his education. Computers. Grammar. Spelling. Fiction written before the 1980s. As far as history went, he knew an Assyrian recurve from an English longbow, but that was about it. Clint could calculate math problems in his head, though, and he understood basic physics. That went along with making sure your arrow hit its target.

"Just remember, we're supposed to check in with the new special officer at 1400." Jessica turned back to her own work.

Clint pretended to focus on his computer screen, punching in letters at random while he watched Red out of the corner of his eye. She had slipped into an empty seat and was typing something into the computer, which instantly responded. That was interesting. She must already know the level-three passwords. Maybe he was wrong about Red. After all, it wasn't as if she could just stroll past a security guard to get into S.H.I.E.L.D. headquarters. That was one of the advantages to having a base of operations that was constantly mobile and usually six miles off the ground.

Red pulled up a schematic of the Helicarrier. Clint told himself there were all kinds of reasons an agent might do that. Maybe she was new to the job and simply trying to locate the ladies' room. She could be a techie from engineering, looking for some faulty wiring. Yeah, and maybe she was searching for decorating tips so she could redo her living room in neo-futuristic polished glass and steel.

Suddenly, the idea of Red being a foreign agent seemed a bit more plausible.

Jessica leaned over. "I take it you meant to write 'redhead' under 'purpose of trip'?"

"Don't tell me you're anti-ginger, Jess."

"Don't call me Jess, *Hawkeye*."

Usually, Clint would retaliate for the use of his old performing name, but he didn't have the time right now. Red was strolling toward the stairs that led down to the flight deck. *All right, show time.* Clint rolled his stool back from the desk and unsnapped a button on his right shoulder, making it easier to reach for the Stark-engineered bow he wore folded on his back. Clint was supposed to wear a regulation firearm like everyone else, but he knew he could snap his wrist and have the recurve primed and ready before another agent could aim and shoot a gun.

"You going somewhere?" Jessica sounded hopeful.

"To see a man about a dog." Red disappeared behind two technicians, and it took Clint a couple of moments to find her again. Did she know he'd made her, or did she always walk in a zigzag pattern, just to be safe?

"Want me to go with you?"

"To the head? Not really." Clint reached for the quiver he always kept propped against his desk, only to find that it wasn't where he'd left it.

"Uh-huh. And what are you planning to do, shoot the soap puck out of the urinal?" Jessica was holding his quiver just out of reach.

"Only if it annoys me." He held out his hand.

"You know, you don't really need to practice shooting things," said Jessica. "You need to practice doing expense reports."

She must be as bored with the paperwork as I am, thought Clint. Probably why she was the closest thing he had to a friend in this place. Looking past Jessica, he widened his eyes. "What the—why is Iron Man flying around without his pants on?"

Jessica turned, and Clint swiped his quiver just as Red reached the exit. She looked over her shoulder; for a moment, their eyes met. A jolt ran through him, the kind he used to feel before doing some trick that was liable to leave him seriously injured or worse if he screwed it up. Red smiled—her hand on the door, as if daring him to follow her—and then she was gone.

"I can't believe it. You're actually leaving a week's worth of forms in order to go hook up with that redhead." Jessica sounded amused rather than offended.

"Depends on your definition of hooking up." Clint swiftly thought through the best arrowheads to bring to this party: magnetic, net, smoke, bola? Selecting the points with capture rather than killing in mind, he inserted them into the automatic loader in his quiver.

"I thought you didn't date co-workers." Now Jessica did sound offended.

"I don't," said Clint, breaking into a run. Around him, heads turned, and a guy in a suit said, "Agent Barton, don't forget you agreed to talk to me about..." but Clint was out the door and charging down the stairs, so he never heard the rest of the sentence.

Clint could hear footsteps on the stairs below him. He was so focused on estimating how far ahead his target was he nearly ran into Agent Coulson, who was carrying a stack of files.

"Slow down there, Barton," said Coulson, nearly dropping his papers. "You know the rules about running in the ladders." Like a lot of paper-pushers, Coulson always used proper Naval terminology.

"Sorry, Coulson." Clint grabbed the staircase railing and vaulted down onto the next landing. "Kind of in a rush, here."

"And you're not wearing sleeves again, Barton," Coulson added. "We've talked about that."

"Later," said Clint, already turning the corner. He had a sudden sense of danger, but it came a second too late, and Clint took the full force of a boot in his face. He managed to recover in time to get another kick to the stomach, this one a roundhouse. God, she was fast—already running down the stairs and nearly at the next landing. Clint flicked his wrist and his bow unfolded.

"Hey, what's the big hurry?" Clint called after her, nocking his arrow and aiming it. "I thought we could spend a little time on small talk before getting down to the dirty stuff."

"I'm not a big fan of small talk," she called back as Clint sent a blunt arrow flying. The arrow hit the pressure point on the back of her leg, just below her knee; for a moment, Clint thought she was going to fall down the stairs. He raced toward her, but Red was already recovering with a neat little backflip. She landed on her feet, lithe as any big-top acrobat.

"I was kind of hoping to get your number before you run off again," said Clint, joining her on the landing. He was too close to aim an arrow now, so he held his bow loosely in his left hand, ready to use it as a blunt instrument if she went for the gun at her hip.

Red appeared bemused. "Do you always talk this much when you're fighting?"

"Not just when I'm fighting, sweetheart. I find talking always adds to the—ungh." Clint moved just in time, so Red's knee connected with his stomach instead of more sensitive parts. He grabbed her foot and she kicked up, wrapping her other leg around his neck and bringing him down on his back, hard. "Okay, now this is definitely a second-date kind of move," he said, maneuvering so he could jab his elbow into the back of her knee, releasing her chokehold on his neck.

"Not so much a second-date kind of girl," she said, straddling him and landing a solid punch to his jaw.

"Still, don't you think I should know your first name?" Clint leveraged his weight, reversing their positions. It seemed a shame to punch that mouth, so Clint just pinned her down, immobilizing her with his arms and legs.

"Sorry, but I don't think this relationship is going anywhere." The woman flexed her wrists; underneath his palms, Clint felt her bracelets grow warm for an instant. Before he could react, a jolt of electricity sent him flying. When he came to, there was a metallic taste in his mouth and Red was gone.

Damn it. Clint shook his head, trying to clear it, then checked his watch. He hadn't been out of commission for more than a minute, so she couldn't have gotten far. He just had to think through the likeliest direction to pursue.

He was one flight of stairs down from the bridge,

on the same level as flight-deck control. Clint couldn't see his unauthorized redhead going in there: The room was windowless and small and hard to enter undetected. For a moment, Clint considered going in there to alert Deputy Director Maria Hill that they had an intruder on board, but then another thought occurred to him. The hangar bay was on this level, too, and it was a huge area filled with fighter planes, jeeps and other Army vehicles. If Red had sabotage on her mind, the hangar bay was a gremlin's paradise.

Clint readied his bow as he ran, heading for the open metal stairs that led to the steel walkway. Some people had a fear of heights, but Clint was always most comfortable perched where he could get a bird's-eye view of the situation. He reached the walkway and quickly scanned as much as he could see of the room below. The hangar bay was basically a big garage, but instead of old cars and discarded toys it contained billions of dollars worth of Uncle Sam's best fighter jets. Parked just below Clint's booted feet, there were a couple of F/A-18 Hornets, which could fight in the air or take out targets on the ground. A little farther away, there was an F-14 Tomcat. Something about the shape of the Tomcat's cockpit reminded Clint of the paper airplanes he used to make when the circus English tutor was droning on about the subjunctive. Clint's namesake plane, the E-2C Hawkeye, was mainly used to relay information on the enemy's position and activity, but its propellers made Clint think of old World War II movies.

No sign of Red. Clint continued scanning the

room, tracking with his arrow. *There.* He caught a flash of movement, darting between a Seahawk helicopter and an S-3B Viking. Hell, that was a subsonic jet capable of taking out a submarine. If Red started messing around in there, she could bring the whole damn Helicarrier crashing down.

Of course, a misplaced arrow could have the same effect. Good thing I don't miss, Clint thought, as he sent his arrow flying. It hit the deck right in front of Red and released its cartridge of tear gas. Since she'd been careful not to inflict any lasting damage on him, he was going to try to return the favor.

But Red had rolled free and grabbed hold of the bottom of the walkway. With a kick of her legs, she brought herself up onto his level. It wouldn't have gotten a 10 from the Olympic judges—her feet were too far apart—but it was pretty elegant, all the same. "I should warn you—it takes a lot to make me cry," she said.

"Tough girl, huh?" But while she had been in motion, Clint had been moving, too, manipulating the joystick on his quiver, selecting a specialized head to cap the shaft of his next arrow. Now he had the arrow nocked and ready, and the bowstring pulled taut. "This arrow contains a hypodermic with a powerful sedative. I suggest you put your hands up, unless you're in the mood for a little nap."

Red's smile was gently mocking. "If you stare a little harder at my equipment, you might notice I'm wearing body armor."

"I noticed. Sorry to disappoint you, but arrows go through Kevlar."

"It's not Kevlar. It's Vibranium."

Clint raised his eyebrows. "Isn't that a little uncomfortable?" Vibranium wasn't exactly standard issue for anyone, even a S.H.I.E.L.D. agent. Rare and extremely expensive, it was one of the few metals that could withstand super-powered levels of force.

"You get used to it." Quick as a cat, she spun and raced down the walkway away from him. A moving target might have posed a challenge for a different archer, but Clint had been shooting things on the fly since he was six. Tucking the hypodermic arrow into his waistband, he toggled the joystick on his quiver, selecting four new arrowheads. Within seconds, he had the first arrow nocked and sent it flying, followed by three more in rapid-fire succession. The arrows, made of Adamantium and equipped with powerful magnetic tips, passed through the taut fabric at Red's wrists and ankles, pinning her against the metal bulkhead so she was standing in the shape of an "X."

"Well, you've drawn first blood," said his opponent, indicating a thin scratch on the exposed part of her wrist where the arrow had grazed her as it went through the fabric of her jumpsuit.

"Unintentional. I only had a millimeter or two to play with. You had the first knockout, though." Clint pulled out the hypodermic-tipped arrow. "Before I go ahead and put you down for the count, mind telling me what you're doing here?"

"Testing your defenses."

"If you're trying to tell me that S.H.I.E.L.D. sent you as some kind of in-house safebreaker, it won't wash. That's what they've got me for."

"I know. You're the one I was testing."

Clint shook his head. "You knew that out of a room filled with over fifty agents, I would happen to be the one to notice you?"

The woman smiled at him. "Absolutely...Hawkeye."

Clint grew still. "Who sent you?" Over the years, he had made some pretty powerful enemies, on both sides of the law.

"I sent myself."

"Not buying it."

"It's the truth. Before I go switching sides, I want to make sure I'm not backing a losing team." She looked up at him, not a hint of coyness in her big, green eyes.

"Your accent is slipping a little."

"I don't have an accent."

"Yeah, you do. It's not so much in the way you pronounce words as it is in the rhythm. I had a Russian guy teach me acrobatics for a while. He moved to the States when he was seven. No accent, but when he got tired, the rhythm of his speech changed."

"You have a good ear." She smiled as if she were his teacher and he had just performed well on a test. That was a hell of a smile she had. Most men probably did a lot of stupid things for one of those. And she probably gutted them with a stiletto without changing her expression.

"So what are you, G.R.U.? S.V.R.?"

"I was *spetsnaz*. Emphasis on was."

"Special ops? You mean black ops?"

She didn't respond, and for the first time Clint knew she wasn't just playing him. She was making up

her mind. For a fraction of a second, there was a worried crease between her eyebrows, and then she ner-
vously licked her lips. "Can I trust you?"

It was the first wrong move Clint had seen her
make. Clint looked down at her, letting her see his
wariness, but also giving her a glimpse of how bone-
tired he was of these kinds of games. It was a calculated countermove, to show her he could be brought
over to her side. "I don't know. Can I trust you?"

Something flickered in her eyes, then: surprise.
"You know what?" she said, dropping all pretense of
being ill at ease. "I think perhaps you can."

With this one, you removed one mask only to find another, thought Clint. "Somehow, I doubt that very much."

"You shouldn't. I'm not the enemy here. Do you see
the red 'X' on my bracelet? Look what happens when
I move my wrist like this." A small needle emerged,
glistening with a drop of moisture. "That's a nerve
agent. If I'd wanted to kill you, you'd be dead."

Clint gave an amused snort of laughter. "You got
nerve, Red, I'll give you that."

"And I would have thought you would be a little
more original," she replied, twisting her wrist so that
the needle went back into the bracelet. "This isn't
even my real hair color."

"So," said Clint, pulling the arrows out of the wall to
release her arms, "what do I call you before I bring you
in to be arrested, court-martialed and sent to prison?"

She held out one small gloved hand. "My given
name is Natalia Romanova, but my friends call me
Natasha."

"Take it off."

"Excuse me?"

"The bracelet. And the glove."

Raising her eyebrows, Natasha pulled off the bracelet, along with the black neoprene glove. She placed them carefully on the floor. "See? No concealed weapons. And now you."

Clint pulled off his archer's gauntlet; after a moment's hesitation, he shook the foreign agent's hand. A shiver of electricity went straight down his back, but Clint disregarded it as a momentary distraction. "So what's your next move, Nat? You going to convince me to let you go?"

"I might," said Natasha with a wry smile. "But somehow, I don't think your girlfriend would agree." She gave a nod of her head, indicating Jessica Drew, who was standing just underneath them, her weapon aimed at Natasha's heart.

TWO

"**YOU** move for your gun, and you're dead," said Jessica, holding the semiautomatic in a firm, two-handed grip as she aimed up at her target. Without taking her eyes off the other woman, she added, "Clint, you incredible idiot, do you have any idea whose hand you're holding? I ran a facial-recognition scan on the computer after you left."

Clint closed his grip on Natasha's hand, keeping her from pulling away. "Aw, ma, you're always checking up on me."

"*Durak*," said Jessica, followed by a stream of what sounded like fluent Russian.

"I got 'durak,' but not the rest," said Clint. *Durak* was what his Russian gymnastics coach had called him when he fudged a landing.

"Allow me to translate," said Natasha, releasing his hand and raising both of hers in surrender. "She says that if I hurt you, she will make me pay."

Now this was getting irritating. "Jessica, I had the situation under control."

Jessica shook her head, still keeping Natasha in her sights. "Clint, she's the Black Widow. And she had you so distracted, you didn't even notice I was in the room until she pointed me out."

The Black Widow. And he'd been pulling his punches and shooting to capture as if this were all a demonstration event. Rumor had it that the Black Widow had once set fire to a remote village's only hospital as a diversion. If even half the stories Clint had heard about her were true, he was lucky she hadn't poisoned him back in the stairwell.

"Don't look so surprised," said the Widow. "I did tell you I wasn't a second-date kind of girl."

Clint wondered whether she remembered her victims' faces, the way he did. "You left out the part where the first date ends with the guy laid out on a slab in the morgue. Hands behind your back."

"This really isn't necessary," said Natasha, bringing her arms behind her as requested. "I told you, Clint, I didn't come here to spy on you."

Clint secured the Black Widow's wrists with his bolo. "Save the explanations for Commander Hill." He didn't know why he should be feeling disappointed that his sparring partner had turned out to be Stalin in a skirt. He tried not to think about the moment when their hands had touched, the way he had reacted like a goddamn kid. He took the gun from her holster and slipped it into his waistband, but decided against patting her down.

"I'd rather talk to you first," said the Widow. "For security reasons."

Clint ignored her. "Jessica? I've got her secured." He drew the string on his bow. "Just so you know, this arrow doesn't do anything fancy. You make a wrong move, I'm going to kill you, plain and simple."

"And I'll kill you again, just to be safe," said Jessica, keeping her gun trained on the other woman. Touching her earpiece, she said, "Commander Hill? We have a contained security breach in the hangar bay involving an unauthorized foreign agent on board the ship." She paused, listening, and then said, "Affirmative. Bringing her in. Have additional guards posted." Looking up, she said, "All right, take her down, nice and easy."

"Turn around and start walking," said Clint, keeping his arrow aimed at the back of Black Widow's head, since the rest of her was armored. When they had reached the hangar floor, Jessica stepped in back of the Widow, gun trained between her shoulder blades.

"Aim higher," said Clint as they made their way through the maze of fighter jets and jeeps. "She's wearing Vibranium."

"Which you know because I told you," Natasha pointed out. "So you see, I didn't have to let you take me in," she told Jessica.

"Shut up and keep moving," said Jessica. "Why the hell didn't you tell me that you were going after her, Clint?"

He shrugged. "Didn't think I needed backup."

"We're supposed to be partners!"

"I've had the same trouble in the field, working with male agents," said Natasha. "Some of them can be such cowboys."

Jessica's lips thinned. "I thought I told you to stop talking."

"I wonder why you seem to dislike me so much," said Natasha. "I mean, on the face of it, we two have quite a lot in common," she went on, as if musing out loud. "I've been called the Black Widow, you've been called Spider-Woman—both arachnids. And of course, you used to be called Arachne, back when you worked for Hydra."

Clint tried to control his surprise. He'd looked up Jessica when they started working together, and he knew about her troubled childhood and the medical treatments her father had given her. He knew that when she had first gotten her powers, Jessica had accidentally killed the first boy she had ever loved. He even knew how Jessica had lost her powers in a fight with a psychotic mutant, and that tidbit was supposed to be classified and out of his security-clearance level. But Clint had never suspected that his partner had once belonged to a terrorist organization.

"Perhaps," said Natasha, "it is simply a case of what Freud called the narcissism of small differences. You dislike me because we are more similar than not."

Jessica glared at the Black Widow's back. "You know, I can just shoot you now and spare Commander Hill the trouble of executing you." They had reached the doors that led to flight-deck control. As if on cue, six agents in full protective battle gear opened the doors and lined up, all training their sights on one unarmed redhead.

The Black Widow didn't bat an eyelash. "You won't kill me. I'm too valuable a source of information. Besides, you wouldn't shoot me for saying the truth, would you?"

"Honey," said Jessica, "at this point, I'd shoot you for saying, 'Have a nice day.' But you're right, I'll do it after we see Commander Hill, just in case she feels like torturing you first."

COMMANDER Maria Hill wasn't happy. She'd been standing in the cramped, windowless launch-operations room all morning, smelling the handler's stale breath as the two of them had attempted to figure out how to manage the imminent arrival of four more Viking jets on the already-crowded flight deck. There was a possible situation brewing in the Middle East and another one exploding in one of the 'stans. And even though Maria was getting better at using Tony Stark's three-dimensional interface screen, she missed the old tabletop "Ouija board" that allowed you to actually pick up the pieces. Between HQ's screwed-up logistics and her coworker's halitosis, she'd already been getting a headache before Jessica's call.

"And that's when Agent Drew arrived," said Agent Barton, concluding his account of the past hour.

Cosa de mala leche, thought Maria. Nothing Clint had said explained how the hell the Black Widow had managed to infiltrate S.H.I.E.L.D.'s flagship command center. One thing that didn't require explanation was the timing. The Russian must have known that Colonel Fury was off on a mission and decided the Helicarrier was an easier target without him around. Maria resisted the urge to rub her right temple, which felt as though someone had tightened a vise around her skull.

"Okay, Ms. Romanova," she said, "let me get this straight. You're telling me that you've left your former organization. Setting aside the question of why the S.V.R. would just permit one of their most effective covert operatives to saunter off into the sunset, do you care to enlighten us as to why you decided on this career switch?"

"They were lying to me."

Maria walked around the Russian woman, trying to get a read on her. She was extremely pretty, and she knew how to use her looks to manipulate men. Would she respond to the threat of disfigurement? Somehow, Maria didn't think so. This woman radiated a kind of cool ruthlessness that would be difficult, if not impossible, to undermine. "Doesn't being lied to come with the territory, Ms. Romanova?"

The Black Widow met Maria's gaze. "Do you lie to your subordinates, Commander Hill? Or do you simply tell them when they are not supposed to ask questions?"

Maria nodded. "You have a point," she conceded. Out of the corner of her eye, Maria watched the two agents who had brought Romanova in. Agent Drew was trying to keep it professional, but from the way she was looking at the Russian, it was clear that Black Widow had gotten under Jessica's skin. Maria wondered whether Clint Barton had anything to do with that. Like Jessica, Barton was an outsider, and it was clear the two agents were friends as well as partners. Were they more than that, or did Jessica want there to be more? Maria wasn't sure. With his blunt features and overgrown crew cut, Clint was certainly no poster boy, but he had a forthright, masculine quality that might appeal to some women. He also looked like the kind of guy who had grown up knowing how to hot-wire a car, secure a bottle of tequila and break into a locked house. Unlike Jessica, Clint had never had superpowers to fall back on, which meant he had spent a lifetime honing his other abilities.

"Commander, if I may make a suggestion," said Jessica, but Maria held up her hand.

"I'm not looking for any more input," she said. "Either this woman is working for the S.V.R., or she's gone rogue. Either way, she managed to infiltrate the Helicarrier and poses a considerable security risk." Jessica opened her mouth and Maria held up her hand again. "On the other hand, she also possesses extremely valuable information. I want her taken down to the Raft for questioning."

Clint nodded, as if he had been anticipating this. The Raft was where prisoners were placed when a maximum-security penitentiary like Ryker's just wasn't secure enough. Situated on an island near Ryker's, the Raft contained eight levels of Adamantium-lined underwater cells and enough fail-safes that Manhattan's citizens didn't worry about the inhumanly powerful psychopaths on their doorstep.

"Agent Drew, Agent Barton, you will accompany Ms. Romanova to the secure holding cell along with an armed escort. From there, she will be placed in additional restraints before being taken to a helicopter for transport. You two will be in charge of the questioning."

The Black Widow kept her poker face. "Come on," said Jessica, but as Clint moved to follow her, Maria gave him an almost imperceptible shake of her head.

"Agent Barton, can you remain behind? I want to speak with you for a moment." Jessica gave him a sympathetic look as she exited the room with her prisoner, clearly under the impression that her partner was about to be reprimanded. The Black Widow also glanced back at him, but Clint acted as though he didn't notice. *Good.* When the door closed, Maria waited a moment before speaking.

"It wasn't exactly the brightest move to take on an unidentified intruder on your own, you know."

To his credit, Clint said nothing.

"On the other hand, it was you who spotted the Black Widow. So I'm giving you the ultimate responsibility, Agent Barton. I'm putting out a call for you to be joined by a S.H.I.E.L.D. consultant with superpowers, as per regulations, but you're in charge. Get every bit of information you can out of her, by any means you deem effective." Maria paused. "But if at any point you think Romanova poses any kind of a threat, or if she shows any signs of attempting to escape, neutralize her."

Clint looked slightly startled by this. "Is that really necessary, ma'am? She's hardly going to be able to overpower both of us and someone with super-powers."

"She shouldn't have been able to break into a top military command center that's been in flight for the past two weeks."

Clint nodded. "Understood." He saluted, then turned to leave.

"Agent Barton. Let me remind you that there is no telling what information the Black Widow may have acquired while roaming around up here."

Clint remained by the door, his back to her. "I am aware of that risk."

"So you understand why she can't be allowed to leave S.H.I.E.L.D. custody. You know her record, Agent. This isn't someone who's just made a couple of bad choices. This is a woman who is up to her neck in innocent blood."

Clint turned, his face set and hard. "Is this an order to take her out no matter what she does or says? 'Cause I don't like it, Commander."

"I don't like it either, Agent Barton. But I don't think she can be turned, and she certainly can't be allowed to roam free. What choice does that leave us?"

A muscle spasmed in Clint's jaw, and then he gave a short nod. "Am I dismissed now?"

"You are."

At the last moment, Clint hesitated with his hand

on the doorknob, looking back over his shoulder. "One last question. May I ask why you chose me for this particular assignment?"

Maria Hill took a deep breath, and then gave him the truth. "Because I watched Romanova while you were talking, Agent Barton, and I think she likes you. I believe she is under the impression that you two have struck up some kind of rapport. And that gives you a little advantage. Unless, of course, she is correct and you think you might have trouble neutralizing the threat she presents?"

Clint didn't hesitate. "I can do it."

Maria nodded and watched him leave. Once she was alone, she closed her eyes and pressed her knuckles into her right eye. This was going to be one hell of a migraine, she thought.

Wonder what Fury would say if he came back to find I'd accidentally taken out my eyeball. Imagining the two of them with matching black patches, Maria had to laugh, which only made her head hurt more.

THREE

NATASHA tried to get a read on Hawkeye as he helped her step down from the Seahawk helicopter. His touch was firm and impersonal as he guided her past the propeller blades and out into the open. It had gotten dark, so it was harder to make out a lot of detail, but Natasha could see the lights of Manhattan twinkling in the distance. She remembered a scene from the movie *Working Girl*, with a young, bright-eyed Melanie Griffith sailing off on her ferry in search of the glass slipper that would crack the glass ceiling. That film had been included in a Red Room Initiative course called "Understanding American Popular Culture: Selling the American Dream."

"What are we doing just standing here?" Hawkeye scanned the empty expanse of concrete. "I thought we needed to get her to the Raft." Despite the chill of the late-November night, he was still dressed in his sleeveless black technical vest, carrying his recurve

bow and quiver on his back. There were six armed
guards in full combat gear looking down the noses of
their sleek, German-made UMP submachine guns.
Jessica Drew also had her weapon cocked and ready,
but it was Hawkeye who remained closest to Natasha,
keeping her in his line of vision at all times.

So he's in charge of me, she thought. She was surprised. She would have expected Commander Hill to
have chosen Jessica Drew, instead. Most people assumed that an attractive female agent would find it
more difficult to manipulate another heterosexual
woman. They were not entirely wrong, although Natasha knew countless strategies for handling a potential asset. Still, attraction was a powerful tool, which
begged the question of why Commander Hill had
chosen this man—especially since Clint had already
demonstrated his fondness for a little cat-and-mous-
ing around. Commander Hill must have been under
the impression the attraction would work both ways.

Hill was not entirely mistaken, but that was beside
the point. Natasha could disregard attraction as easily
as she could ignore hunger or fatigue, or pain. And if
he felt something for her, the man they called Hawkeye certainly wasn't showing it.

"We have to follow S.H.I.E.L.D. protocol, Clint,"
Jessica Drew said.

"Which involves standing around for half an hour.
What's the idea, we trying to build up suspense?"

Jessica shook her head. "Commander Hill said we
wait for a super-powered agent to escort us in." Unlike Hawkeye, Jessica had donned a short military

jacket with the S.H.I.E.L.D. eagle emblem discreetly embossed on the fabric.

"Yeah, well, super-powers are overrated, if you ask me."

Jessica smiled at him. "Spoken like a man who's never had them."

There was no hint of bitterness in the other woman's voice. *Interesting.* Natasha had read the woman's file and had thought she was far less resigned to the loss of her former powers. It reminded Natasha of another American film, about a young woman who acquires a roommate who copies her haircut, borrows her clothes and seduces her boyfriend—and then tries to kill her. That movie had also been part of a course called "Maintaining Identity While Adopting An Assumed Persona."

Natasha still hadn't decided who to be during the questioning. While sparring with Hawkeye, she had considered and discarded a few possibilities: the amoral adventurer, the lethal foundling, the hedge knight in search of a benefactor. She thought he could be seduced, but not by anything obvious. *Never mind.* It would come to her in time. It always did.

Hawkeye rolled his shoulders, loosening the muscles. "Any idea who they're sending?"

"Luke Cage," said Jessica, looking at her phone. "I just got a text saying he'll be here in a few minutes."

This was another piece of information that might prove useful. Natasha tried to recall what she knew about Cage. He was called Power Man in the press, but Natasha couldn't recall exactly what those powers were. She knew he had been born and raised in Harlem, and that he had been sent to prison for a crime he hadn't committed. He had gotten his powers while incarcerated, the result of an attempt to recreate the Super-Soldier serum that had produced Captain America during World War II.

The sound of a small boat engine grew louder, and Natasha guessed she was about to meet Luke Cage in person. As they waited, she felt a moment's fleeting regret that she couldn't just hop on the boat herself and explore Manhattan. She had only been to New York once before, but that had been for a quick in-and-out assassination, so she hadn't seen anything except the airport and a hotel room. *The curse of the business traveler.*

As the boat docked, Natasha took a more careful look at her surroundings. They were standing in an outdoor parking lot, next to a large rocky outcropping, a vestige of the island's glacial past. Beside it, there was a large, shadowy building with a gloomy, industrial appearance. It might have been an old warehouse, or one of those discarded buildings where bureaucrats from the previous century had checked new immigrants for parasites and diseases.

No, she realized. It was neither. This must be the top level of the Raft. She had read accounts of the prison's construction back in Russia, but there had been no pictures of the facility. Natasha made a careful note of the windows and doors, and the distance to the East River, in case she should need to make a quick exit.

As she turned back to the others, she saw Luke Cage stepping out of the boat. He moved with surprising grace, considering his size. As he approached their group, Jessica stepped forward. It was clear from the way she greeted him that she had met Cage before, and that the two were on friendly terms. Natasha could detect no sign of the tensions she had read about in her course on "Racial Stereotyping and the Psychological Legacy of Slave-Ownership in North America." Perhaps super-powered people all hung out together to talk shop, like stockbrokers or safebreakers or models.

Luke Cage turned to look at Natasha, and inclined his head. "*Zdrastvotyeh*," he said. Unlike the other two agents, Cage wasn't in uniform. Instead, he wore a gray wool hat, a black leather jacket and dark chinos. He didn't need a uniform to appear intimidating, however. He was easily six-foot-four and padded with so much muscle that he resembled an American football player. In addition, the close-cropped black goatee gave him a slightly sinister look.

"Do you speak Russian?" she asked him, in that language.

"*Nimnoshka*," he replied. "The grammar drives me crazy."

"It drives schoolchildren crazy in Russia, too," she said, smiling. He was not what she had expected.

"Ask her to tell you about all the children in the hospital in Urus-Martan," said Jessica, in English, presumably so Clint would understand what she was saying.

Natasha couldn't prevent a momentary stiffening of her muscles as she recalled the little girl's hopeful expression. *Are you here to save us, Miss?* Natasha glanced at Clint and saw that he had noted her involuntary reaction to Jessica's gibe. *If you make a mistake, do it twice and make it seem deliberate.* Natasha averted her gaze, letting him see that Jessica had scored a point.

Luke shook his head and said something in Jessica's ear that made her laugh. "Come on," he said, addressing the group in a deep, resonant baritone. "Why don't we head on down into the Raft?"

Nicely phrased, thought Natasha, as if I had a choice. She took a last look at the Manhattan skyline that reminded her of old Hollywood movie propaganda, then followed Luke Cage into the building. Behind her, she could feel Hawkeye's quiet presence. As she stepped into one of the world's most impenetrable fortresses, surrounded by criminals who could teleport through walls or melt steel with their breath or kill with a thought, Natasha felt curiously reassured that a man with a bow and arrow was there to watch her back.

THE Raft had been built to address the problem of incarcerating prisoners who looked at armed guards the way Labrador retrievers look at tennis balls. Like New York's subway tunnels, the Raft had been constructed underground, but far deeper, beneath the East River.

As they made their way down a long hallway, past the fluorescent glare of the lights and the rock walls,

Natasha noticed a large, presumably bulletproof glass window on their left. Behind the glass, she could see a number of guards observing different screens. The screens displayed various locations around the prison, including the hallway. Natasha caught a glimpse of herself, followed closely by Clint, his bow held loosely in his left hand. Glancing up, Natasha could see cameras trained on them, red lights flickering as the lenses tracked their progress.

"There appear to be no windows to the outside," she observed out loud. "That must be difficult for the prisoners." She was wondering whether any of their little group had any problem with claustrophobia.

"It's a necessary precaution," said Jessica. "Because of the abilities of the inmates, the walls here are lined with either Adamantium or Vibranium. There's no way to reinforce glass to that degree."

"Understandable. Still, I would rather spend my life in a Siberian work camp than live without a window," said Natasha, giving a little shiver at the thought of spending one sunless day after another.

"Cut it out," said Clint, following behind her.

"Cut what out?"

"The vulnerable act."

"You so sure it's an act?" Luke Cage fell back to walk beside Clint. "I kind of agree with her. I was in stir for over three years, but at least we got to go out in the yard for some fresh air. This place? They're buried alive. I got to admit, that creeps me out."

"So maybe she's a method actress. It's still an act."

This was so astute that Natasha realized she had

been underestimating the archer. Perhaps he had picked up more than just athletic skills during his circus training. Then, glancing up, she noticed a series of openings in the metal wall ahead. "Aren't those windows?" She had to gather as much information as possible about this place, as it could prove extremely valuable should she decide to return to Russia. *Assuming I don't move in here permanently, of course.*

"Those are video screens," said Jessica, her heels clicking on the floor. "And they're two-way. Unlike some countries I can name, the United States attempts to treat its prisoners with as much humanity as possible."

Clint and Cage exchanged glances. "You've never been in lockup, have you, Jessica?"

Jessica looked over her shoulder. "Look, I'm not saying that prison is fun. It's not supposed to be fun. Do you have any idea what these inmates have done? What they're capable of doing?"

"He doesn't look capable of much," said Luke, nodding at the first video screen. It showed a large man with a small, pointy head crouched in the corner of his cell. Pale brown fur covered most of his body, and he was dressed in a rumpled white T-shirt and pants that reminded Natasha of something a mental patient might wear. He looked like a cross between a circus freak and a rat. He looked up, wrinkling his nose, his small, bright eyes following them as they walked by.

"Who is that?"

"Vermin. He has limited intelligence, but he's very fast and extremely strong," said Jessica.

The next video screen showed an even more disturbing face. This prisoner had the swollen blue cheeks and bright-red, doglike muzzle of an adult male baboon, but his golden eyes had a distinctly human shape. Dressed in a denim work shirt and jeans, the prisoner appeared to be sitting at his desk and reading a book. On closer inspection, Natasha saw that the title was *Extraordinary Delusions and the Madness of Crowds*.

"What is this," said Luke, "the crimes-against-nature section?"

"I think they're classified according to threat level," said Jessica. "That's Mandrill. His given name is Jerome Beechman, and his parents were both physicists working in Gabon." After an almost imperceptible pause, she added, "There was an accident in the lab."

Natasha recalled that Jessica had received her powers in a similar fashion, but that was hardly unusual. Most super-powered individuals were either born with mutant abilities, or had acquired them in some sort of lab experiment. Iron Man was one of the rare exceptions.

"His parents deserted him at age ten," said Jessica. "They just drove him off into the middle of an unpopulated bit of forest and left him there, along with a girl a little older than himself."

"That's cold," said Luke. "Where's the girl now?"

Jessica's smile was a bit rueful. "With that start in life? She wound up in here, as well."

"So the women are housed separately?" It would do Natasha no good to memorize the floor plan here, if this was not where she would be incarcerated.

"Yes," Jessica began, but stopped as Luke let out a low curse.

"Purple Man," he said, as they passed a screen showing an aristocratically handsome man in his early thirties with a distinctly violet skin tone. The way Luke said his name sounded worse than the expletive that had preceded it. "As far as threat level goes, this guy should be buried in the deepest cell in this place."

"Zebediah Killgrave," said Natasha. "I know of him. He is from Rijeka, in Croatia. Is it safe to allow him to watch us like this? I thought he could control thoughts by making eye contact."

Jessica laid a hand on Luke's arm. "He's drugged to the gills, Luke. He doesn't even know where he is. I'm sorry, I didn't think about how you might feel, seeing him."

Despite this assurance, Natasha did not meet the man's deep, heliotrope-colored eyes. Instead, she looked at Luke, who was clearly suppressing some powerful emotion as they walked past Killgrave's cell. "Did he hurt you?"

"That's hardly any of your business," said Jessica.

"Not me," said Luke, clearly not willing to elaborate.

"His wife," said Clint, when Luke had moved a few steps ahead. "Killgrave captured his wife and convinced her…that she wanted to be with him. Then he messed with her head."

"I see," said Natasha. "That is, I think, the worst kind of abuse. I would prefer physical pain to psychological torture."

Clint didn't say anything.

"I thought you liked to talk," she said as they reached an elevator.

"Guess I kind of lost the mood," he said, gesturing for her to go in before him. "After you."

Natasha walked into the elevator and tried not to think about whether she would be making the return trip. She understood now that, in all probability, she would not. Read bodies and faces, her old instructor, Svetlana Bobkova, had always told her. She could still see the woman's calm, round face, so deceptively maternal as she taught the young girl how to lie and how to detect lies.

Natasha had learned it was easiest to lie with words. Our bodies betray us, revealing our true intentions. Natasha had learned to lie with her body, too, but most people could not. She had also learned to read silences. When someone stopped talking to you, it was usually a very bad sign. For most people, killing was not an easy thing. We stop engaging with people because we need to depersonalize them. We depersonalize them so we can kill them.

Natasha stole a glance at Clint's face as the elevator went down and down. The pressure in her ears told her that even though there were only eight buttons, they were plunging quite a distance, and rapidly. *I miscalculated*, she thought. *I was not clear in my own mind about my objective.* She had left her old bosses, but she had not fully embraced the idea of joining the Americans. Infiltrating the Helicarrier had seemed like a way of testing S.H.I.E.L.D.'s defenses, as well as a fine method for demonstrating the extent of her own abilities. Too late, Natasha saw that she had not played the chess game out in her head, the way she had been taught. Her own ambivalence had kept her from fully analyzing her opponents' reactions.

The only question remaining was: Could she learn from this mistake, or would it be her last?

"We're here," said Jessica. "Are you all right? What you said about claustrophobia before—are you having a problem being this far underground?"

"A little," Natasha admitted. She could see no advantage in hiding it, and revealing her vulnerability might well work in her favor.

"Don't believe her," said Clint. "She's too tough for phobias. She's just angling for an advantage."

Irritated, Natasha stiffened her spine. "Let's get this over with," she said, as the doors slid open. Taking a deep breath, she stepped out into a long hallway hewn out of rock. *It's like some sort of gnome kingdom.* A chill of fear swept through her at the thought that she might really never see the sun or feel the air on her face again.

She took a step backward and felt something sharp bite into her left shoulder. An arrowhead.

"Careful, Red," said Clint.

The tiny pain helped clear her head a little. "I am always careful," she lied.

"Nobody's always careful," he said, "least of all, you." For a moment, Natasha heard a hint of the playful, teasing tone from their sparring match in the Helicarrier. And then it hit her. *He responds to me when I speak or act without careful calculation.* In order to manipulate Clint Barton, Natasha would have to be herself. *But do I even know who that is, anymore?*

She thought of the punishing final week of Black Widow training at the Red Room facility, and how she had foolishly told her roommate, Yelena, that they were like sisters. Yelena, blonde hair damp from the shower, had looked at her with something like pity in her cool gray eyes. "We are not sisters, Natasha. We are not even friends. How could we be? Tell me, what is your favorite movie? Your favorite author? What would you wear to go out to a party if you were not on assignment? You don't know, because you are always on assignment, or preparing for one. But if I asked you your favorite weapon, you could tell me that, yes? You know how you like to kill."

Yelena had spoken out of jealousy and resentment, but it was all true. Natasha had no idea who she was when she wasn't manipulating others, because she had, for so long, been manipulated herself.

"You're awfully quiet," said Hawkeye. "Not hatching any escape plans, I hope."

"No more than usual." *I wonder,* she thought, *if I had met Clint Barton in some normal way, what would have happened?* It did no good to conjecture. She could not even imagine what "some normal way" might involve.

The hallway stretched in front of them, lit by the unnatural glow of fluorescent lights. There were no video screens down here, and the windowless doors of the inmates' cells were fitted with coded keypads. A metallic grate underfoot suggested the possibility of electric shock as a fail-safe for any potential prisoner escape, yet underneath it all Natasha detected the ancient, cool, moist smell of stone and earth shared by caves and catacombs and graves.

"Clint? Would you do me a favor?" Natasha was working on pure impulse now, something she hadn't done since age seven, when Svetlana and her other teachers had shown up at the orphanage.

"Probably not, but you can ask."

"If I'm not going to walk out of here, kill me."

She felt his stillness and understood instantly. *This is what Commander Hill told him, when she called him back to speak alone.*

"I take it you know which room we're supposed to use, Jessica," said Luke Cage. "I'd rather not open up the wrong cell and find myself face to face with…" There was a click, and then the lights went out. "Um…this kind of thing supposed to happen?"

"Not that I'm aware of," said Jessica, sounding very controlled. "Our regular phones won't work down here. Can anyone feel along the wall for the intercom?"

As Jessica and Luke searched for the intercom, they could hear muffled shouts and curses coming from inside the cells.

"Don't get any ideas, Nat." Natasha felt one of Clint's hands close around her arm. Was it there to offer support, because he thought she would be frightened, or to secure her and prevent her from escaping? "There are folks down here scarier than you are."

"Are you sure about that?" Despite everything, she was very aware of his hand on her arm.

His fingers tightened. "Keep your hands away from my weapons."

"Maybe I was reaching for your hand."

"They don't teach anatomy where you come from?"

It's working, Natasha thought. *He is beginning to—*

And then the lights flickered and flared with a crackle of surging power, and a lightning blast of light and energy threw Natasha and Clint back against the wall. An alarm began to blare with the insistent, intermittent rhythm of an animal's distress call. But it was another sound that made Natasha reach for the gun she always carried at her hip, only to recall it wasn't there.

Up and down the dark hallway, cell doors were sliding open.

Behind her, Natasha heard Clint selecting a different arrow from his quiver. He must be doing it by feel, thought Natasha. She couldn't see a thing yet.

"Damn it. If there's no power, why aren't the cells staying locked?"

"Because someone's controlling them," said Natasha, finally able to make out the shapes of things. She pulled an arrow from his quiver. Clint glanced at her, but did not object.

"Jessica," said Luke. "You have a flashlight?"

"Here." She turned the light on, transforming the shadows around them into a sea of unfriendly faces: an enormously obese man with an absurdly tiny head, the kewpie doll mouth pursed in a little smile. A hideous, flat-nosed bat face, gazing at her with bright, unblinking eyes. The green, chiseled gargoyle features of a Skrull, assessing her with alien intelligence.

"*Buzhe moi*," said Natasha.

She was going to die down here, after all, and a lot more quickly than she had anticipated.

FOUR

PETER Parker knew there were times when the only way to survive a bad situation was to accept a certain amount of punishment. Maybe that wasn't true for some: Thor, for example, probably didn't get his ass handed to him on a regular basis. But Thor was an A-list super hero, the kind who got courted by teams like the Avengers. You could tell just by looking at him that Thor had grown up knowing he was first pick for troll-tipping or whatever adolescent Norse gods did for fun.

For your friendly neighborhood Spider-Man, on the other hand, a bit of pain and humiliation came with the territory. Take the time when he'd faced down Dr. Octopus and his army of prosthetic limbs—that had been both agonizing and fairly ridiculous.

Then there were the romantic debacles. Other people made out with the wrong girl and got a big cold sore or maybe a case of mono. Peter had kissed the wrong girl once and turned into a massive, man-eating spider.

Last but not least, there was the breakup with Mary Jane. Peter still couldn't believe that she didn't accept "I was captive and unconscious" as a reasonable excuse for standing her up at the altar. Or, to be more precise, she accepted it, but decided she could no longer accept him, so long as he remained Spider-Man. Sure, he understood her point of view, and yeah, in a way, they were kind of living in different worlds. But if he were to give up the web-slinging lifestyle, what the hell was he supposed to do? Maybe he could start a special upside-down yoga class at the local gym. Or take up weaving spider-silk plant holders.

So in the end, there hadn't really been a choice at all. You couldn't choose the girl at the cost of giving up yourself. Still, at the time, Peter had been pretty certain the breakup with MJ was an all-time low for him.

Now he knew differently.

"There's nothing wrong with a bit of humor," said the humorless blonde woman sitting opposite him on the couch. "The problem is, you use humor as a defense."

Peter tried to look as though he were contemplating the truth of this as he glanced surreptitiously at the clock. Nine o'clock. He had been here for two hours, but it felt like decades had passed.

"I mean, on our last date, you kept making jokes even when we were making out. What does that tell you about yourself?"

That I was having the worst date of my life, thought

Peter. He could no longer even recall how he had ever found this woman attractive. She was wearing a perfume that smelled like cumin and incense, and it made him want to sneeze. All the books in her apartment had titles like *The Self-Actualized Person's Guide to Nutritional Wholeness* and *Milk and Meat: The Politics of Cow.* For dinner, she had served him a vegetable stir-fry without any salt, accompanied by that glorious icebreaker, unsweetened green tea. Worst of all, she had forced him to listen to the first two chapters of her unpublished YA series about a lonely high-school sophomore who discovers she's really the Greek goddess of agriculture.

Peter wondered how much longer he had to remain in Anthea's apartment in order not to give offense. Another half hour? Another hour? Long enough to demonstrate that he was not the kind of sleazeball who got fixed up with a girl, fooled around with her on their first date, and then vanished without a word. The worst part of it all was, she lived and worked in Queens, only a few blocks from him.

"You know, Peter, when you called me back yesterday, I nearly said no to getting together again."

But then I realized that I had not tortured my quota of male souls for the week, thought Peter. Out loud, he made a vague grunting sound meant to simulate interest. There was a pen on the coffee table. Peter picked it up and twiddled it between his fingers.

"I've been traumatized by relationships with boymen in the past, you see."

"Mm." Peter passed the pen under and around his index finger and thumb, the way he used to back in social studies class.

"In fact, before I met you, I was considering becoming celibate."

"I'm considering it now."

"Excuse me?"

"I was engaged to be married not long ago, and I think I may have rushed into dating again." Outside the window, Peter heard the familiar sound of a police siren. From where he sat, he could see the lights in dozens of windows in the building across the street. Each and every person in that building, Peter thought, is having a better evening than I am.

"What are you saying, that I was some kind of rebound fling? That you don't want to see me anymore? And will you please stop fiddling with that pen!"

Looking back at his date's pale, annoyed face, Peter opened his mouth to say something about not feeling terribly well.

Then the lights went out.

"What was that?" Anthea tried to turn on the lamp next to the couch. "Did a fuse blow?"

"I don't think so," said Peter, walking over to the window. He looked past the darkened windows of the building opposite, out toward the East River. There was a sharp crack of thunder, and for a fraction of a second, Peter thought he saw a massive bolt of lightning hit Ryker's Island. Then, as a second lightning strike replaced the first, understanding dawned: This was a feat of engineering, not nature. That enormous surge of electrical energy was either coming *from* the island's prison complex—or, more ominously, from beneath.

"Is it a blackout?" Anthea came up behind him, putting a hand on Peter's shoulder.

"Anthea, do you have a flashlight?"

"Yes, I think so. In the kitchen."

"Can you get it?"

"Sure," said Anthea. "Hang on a moment."

From the other room, Peter heard her say something about "crises that bring people closer together" and "the elemental power of darkness." By that time, he already had his shoes off, revealing the thin, flexible red boots underneath. Luckily, Peter had worn his Spider-Man costume underneath his clothes with the idea of patrolling after he was done with Anthea.

"I couldn't find my flashlight," Anthea said from the other room, "but I did see some candles."

Peter left his shirt and jeans, along with his wallet, in a heap on the living-room floor. She would think it weird, of course, and he would have to face her in the morning to pick up his stuff, but there was nothing to be done about that.

"You know, maybe this is some kind of sign," said Anthea.

"You got that right," Peter muttered under his breath. Crouching on the windowsill, Peter launched himself out into the brisk November night, allowing himself a few moments of free-fall before activating his right web-shooter. He aimed the powerful jet of liquid web-fluid at a building and then felt the familiar tug as the web attached, turning almost instantly into a slender, deceptively strong rope. *How could I ever give this up?* thought Peter as he swung his body forward, pressing his middle finger into his palm to release a second strand of webbing.

Maybe it was wrong to feel a wild rush of elation, given the circumstances. But a minute ago, he had been a loser and a tool, and now he was a man with a mission.

Peter paused at the roof of a building, staring out at Macneil Park, and felt his mood plummet. There were no buildings between here and Ryker's, just a lot of cold East River. *Fardles.* Peter's red-and-blue spider-suit wasn't exactly drip-dry, and he did not relish the thought of trying to swim more than an icy mile out to the island.

Just as Peter was about to head over to the 19th Avenue bridge, he heard the rhythmic *whump-whump* of a helicopter's propellers overhead. *That's my ride,* he thought, and then hesitated, trying to estimate the height. *Ah well, life's for taking chances.* Peter shot out his right arm and flexed his wrist hard, sending the webbing out to attach to the undercarriage.

For a few glorious moments, Peter enjoyed a toll-free trip over the East River. But just as the dock came into sight and the chopper began its descent, there was a crack of thunder and a blast of light that illuminated the sky. A plume of black smoke erupted from the helicopter, and Peter had just enough time to arc his body away from the falling metal before it exploded in a huge fireball.

As he plummeted toward the river, Peter recalled something a friend had said about jumping from a bridge: *Point your feet or you'll break your ankles.* Peter pointed his feet and knifed through the water, shooting straight down for what felt like a very long time. *Maybe I shouldn't have bailed on that date,* thought Peter, as he swam for the surface. All of a sudden, Anthea's apartment didn't seem like such a lousy place.

His lungs felt like they were bursting by the time his head broke the surface. Peter gasped, inhaled a mouthful of foul-tasting water, and gasped again. The water was so cold that it was hard to make his arms and legs move properly. As Peter set off for the dock, or what he hoped was the dock, he heard another crack of thunder, followed by the icy patter of sleet. *Just great. I'll bet this never happens to Iron Man.*

Shivering hard, Peter took two tries to haul himself up out of the frigid water, using the gaps in the metal dock as footholds. In the back of his head, Peter felt the static buzz of his spider-sense reminding him that he was heading straight into some serious badness. *Assuming I survive this,* Peter thought, *I don't even have a ride home.*

Gripping the edge of the dock with numb fingers, Peter chinned himself up high enough to see the orange glow of burning helicopter fragments. Just as he was wondering whether he had the strength to get the rest of his body onto the dock, Peter looked up and saw Captain America, his red-white-and-blue suit torn and a little singed, extending one red-gloved hand out. "I got you," he said, hauling Peter up onto the landing dock.

"Excuse me, Captain," said a S.H.I.E.L.D. agent with a special-ops insignia on his uniform, "but we've secured the perimeter and are working to contain the blaze. A team is donning protective gear and preparing to insert themselves into the facility once the flames are extinguished."

"Roger that, Lieutenant. Are there any guards available?"

"Only two that weren't seriously injured in the blast, sir."

"Well, put them to work. Do we have a map of the area immediately underneath the blast site?"

"No hard copies, and the power's still down."

"Get the guards to draw something you can follow. We don't want to go in there blind."

The S.H.I.E.L.D. agent turned and began barking commands at the other troops.

"Glad to see you here, Spider-Man," said Captain America, turning back to Peter. "As you can see, we're a bit short-handed."

"Well, my evening needed some adrenaline to goose it along," said Peter, noting Cap looked even more heroic with a few rips in his costume. "You don't happen to have any spare gym trunks, do you? I'm soaked to the bone."

"Sorry, this was an unexpected detour. Don't suppose you have any idea what's going on here?"

"Someone's been overusing their ionic hair dryer?" Captain America didn't appear to be amused by this, so Peter tried a different tack. "Look, Cap, I just got here. I was hoping *you* could fill *me* in."

"I see." Captain America turned to survey the men and women spraying the remains of the burning helicopter with fire extinguishers. The steady, sleety rain was working in their favor, and Cap turned his attention to the Raft—or what was visible of it from this angle. The electrical blast had been focused on the building's north side in a small, elevated section of the mainly below-ground prison. There was an enormous, gaping hole in the roof of this section, and the glass in all the windows had been blown out by the force of the explosion. It was clear from cracks in the upper walls there had been some structural damage, but it was impossible to gauge the extent of it from the ground.

"Darn it." Captain America looked grim as he watched an injured agent being dragged away from the blaze toward the makeshift first-aid station. Four guards were already out of commission, receiving oxygen or being treated for blistering second-degree burns. "We need to get in there, and fast."

Cap turned back to Peter, who was working hard to suppress the violent shivers racking his body. Peter could almost hear Cap thinking, Great, *this* is what I have to work with.

"All right, I'll take point, since I've got my shield. Soldier," Cap said to a young man in protective gear, "how many of your men are combat-ready?"

"About twenty. I've got four injured here and six trapped behind a section of fallen roof on the second floor, but no idea what to expect when we get inside.

There's no communication with anyone below level B."

All right, Peter. Time to make yourself useful. Spider-Man was up the side of the two-story building in the time it took him to complete the thought. From this vantage point, the sky and water were identical shades of battleship gray, divided by the black silhouettes of Manhattan's skyline. The wind was blowing the icy rain down at an angle. Against this bleak backdrop, bright-orange flames from the downed helicopter illuminated the Raft's lower dock. There was no sign of the incandescent, blue-white light Peter had seen blasting through the roof.

Down on the ground, Captain America was still making plans. "All right, then, let's break into three groups," he said. "Spider-Man, you can lead…Spider-Man?"

Peter peeked down from the side of the roof. "Already on it."

Captain America shook his head. "I appreciate your initiative, but the last thing we need is to go off half-cocked."

"Funny, that's what my date said." The surface of the roof felt hot and tarry underfoot as Peter made his way toward the deep fissure. "You know, I was under the impression that this whole structure was reinforced with Adamantium and Vibranium. Tch. You just can't trust builders not to skimp on materials."

"Spider-Man, you need to wait for backup!"

Peter walked carefully around the gaping hole in the roof, avoiding the sections that were still smoldering. "I'm not planning on taking the full tour of the underworld on my own. I'm just scouting around up here to get a picture of what's..." Peter paused, peering into the dark, rubble-filled room below. There was no sign of movement, but his skin was prickling as though someone had raked fingernails over a chalkboard. "Whoa. I'm getting a bad feeling here."

"What kind of bad feeling?"

"The kind that says the evening's probably not going to end well."

"I'm coming up," said Captain America.

Suddenly, Peter heard a loud bang. A glowing ball of violet light flew up at him from the hole in the roof—and then there was a second, louder bang, followed by a searing pain that whited out all thought.

When Peter came to, he found himself lying face-down near the fissure, looking down through the twisted shards of metal and crumbled stone. It took him a moment to focus on what he was seeing. When he did, it was like peering down into one of the lowest chambers of Hell: A score or more of malevolent faces stared back at him, features twisted by mutation or cruelty or some combination of the two.

Time seemed to slow down for a second as Peter picked out the villains he recognized: Count Nefaria, elegant and silver-haired and capable of knocking over a tank with just one hand; Armadillo, with his orange-plated exterior; Crusher Creel, his shiny, bald head and boxer's blunt features frightening even without the absorbing powers that allowed him to take on the attributes of any substance he touched; Max Dillon, who had gotten his hands on his old green-and-yellow Electro costume and was grinning like a middle-grade sociopath with his very own kitten.

"Spider-Man," said Electro. "Don't be shy. Come on down and play with us."

"What is it? What do you see?" Captain America's voice sounded very far away.

"Unfriendlies," said Peter, and then he was being dragged down into the mob. Someone tore off his mask. There were shouts of "Kill him!" Another voice, lower and cultured, said, "No. We can use him as a hostage." Rough hands pulled at him, yanking his arms and legs in opposite directions. A fist slammed into his eye, spangling his vision and scrambling his thoughts. Another blow, this one to his ear, left his head ringing. Electro said, "Wait! My turn!" An electric shock crackled through Peter, making him scream.

When his vision cleared, Peter saw a face, fractured and scarred like a badly put-together jigsaw puzzle.

"Remember me?" The breath smelled raw, like bloody meat. One of the eyes, popped nearly loose of its socket, regarded Peter with sadistic pleasure.

"Did we hook up in driver's ed?" The words came, unplanned, from some reflexive, defiant impulse. Peter knew he'd be regretting them.

"Nice comeback. This is mine."

There was a crack, and Peter felt a pain in his wrist that sent him spiraling down into a foul darkness. It was a bit like falling from the helicopter into the East River. But this time, he didn't come to the surface.

FIVE

CLINT knew that the Raft contained eighty-seven of the world's most dangerous criminals. In the dim glow of the emergency lights along the floor, he could see dozens of them gathered in the corridor, but he consoled himself with the knowledge that they couldn't all attack him at once. *At the most, four guys can go for you at once. Maybe five.* Whichever, four or five guys at once; Clint could handle those odds.

The beam of Jessica's flashlight picked faces out of the gloom. At first glance, the five villains closest to Clint looked normal enough, although looks could be deceiving. Three of them, however, were clearly metahuman. Carnage, the nasty-looking red-and-black creature with the slick assortment of tendrils, was one. The baboon-faced Mandrill was another. And Zebediah Killgrave, as handsome as a movie star and as purple as a violet, was possibly the most dangerous of all.

Luckily, Purple Man still seemed to be under the influence of whatever drug the Raft had been using to keep him from controlling everyone's minds. He was wiggling his fingers and laughing softly to himself.

Just to be safe, Clint chose his arrow and aimed it at Purple Man. The minute Killgrave looked up, Clint was going to take him out.

There was a flicker of light and a hum. *The emergency generators must have come on*, Clint realized.

For a moment, everyone just stood there, like a bunch of kids staring down a rival gang. Violence was in the air, as palpable as the scent of ozone and burnt-out wiring, but everyone seemed to be waiting for some invisible signal.

"Oh, they sent us girls," said Mandrill, looking from Jessica to Natasha with a simian grimace of pleasure. "Let me have the redhead."

"Sorry, ape man, but you're not my type."

"Sweetheart, that's only because my pheromones haven't hit you yet. I've got biological agents in my blood that make me every woman's type."

"I don't mind if you play with the food," said Carnage, waving one of his scarlet tendrils suggestively. "I just claim dibs when you're done."

Killgrave let out a little nervous giggle, and then crouched down in a corner. "Lavender's blue, dilly, dilly," he sang softly to his purple fingers. "Lavender's green. When I am king, dilly, dilly, you'll be my queen."

"Hate to disappoint you boys," said Luke, glancing down at Killgrave before addressing Mandrill and the others, "but this here is actually the high point of your day. You can think back on it when you're back in your cells, betting on which cockroach reaches your toilet first."

"Oh, I don't know about that," said a handsome man with silver at his temples and a faint Italian accent.

Great, Clint thought. *That has to be Count Nefaria.*

"I think your little group is both outnumbered and outclassed."

Jesus, thought Clint, he wasn't kidding. Nefaria had been a crime boss until he had funneled his money into scientific experiments. Now, thanks to a series of ionic-energy treatments, Nefaria was one of the few individuals on the planet who could go mano a mano with Thor.

"Are we? You're nowhere near full strength," said Jessica, "and Gerhardt and Leighton here don't have any weapons handy."

"Lady, I'm Cutthroat, and that's the Foolkiller," said Daniel Leighton. While in prison, he had gotten some clumsy blue tattoos of knives at his throat and on his forearms. "We don't need weapons."

"We *are* weapons," said Kurt Gerhardt. Clearly, thought Clint, the two had become close in prison.

A long-faced man with thick glasses stepped forward. "And God is on our side, you raven-haired trollop." Clint assumed this was Arthur Blackwood, also known as the Crusader.

Jessica looked at Clint. "Why does he assume that I'm a trollop? Have I done anything particularly trollopy?"

Clint shrugged. "Maybe it's your outfit."

Jessica turned back to the Crusader, pointing her thumb at Clint. "His outfit's just as tight as mine. And *his* has no sleeves."

Blackwood pushed his glasses up on his nose. "Speak not to me, foul harlot! My faith empowers me, and I will not be tempted by your lascivious flesh!"

The unfortunate thing was, Blackwood's faith really did empower him. He held out his right hand, produced a sword out of thin air, and then lunged at Jessica. As if this were the moment they had all been waiting for, everyone moved at once, some attacking, some running away.

Luke Cage plowed a path through the inmates, his powerful fists feinting and jabbing while he rocked quickly from foot to foot, never staying in the same place for more than an instant. Natasha, seeing a chance to use the man's bulletproof body as a shield, followed him, kicking with lethal grace whenever she saw an opening.

Luke won't let her get away, Clint reassured himself as he nocked an arrow in his bow. A grinning inmate with an odd, melted look to his skin tried to grab Clint's arm. Clint knocked him out with his elbow and continued drawing his bow.

He caught a movement out of the corner of his eye: Blackwood was driving Jessica back at swordpoint. "Have at you, wanton! You think to fill my mind with lustful cravings, but I will prevail!"

"Guess those prison therapy sessions didn't help much," said Jessica, aiming her gun at Blackwood's hand.

"Psychiatrists are the tools of—ow!" The Crusader clutched his shoulder, dropping his sword, as the bullet struck his arm. "Ow!" Suddenly he looked crestfallen. "My God, how have I offended thee?"

"Maybe She didn't like you calling me a trollop," said Jessica, already taking aim at a new threat. "Clint, Nefaria's getting away!"

Clint let four arrows fly in rapid succession, pinning the older man to the wall with the same Adamantium-reinforced magnetic arrows he had used on the Black Widow earlier that day.

Unlike the Widow, Nefaria broke free of them with infuriating ease.

"*Scusi*, my friend, but I think I broke your toothpicks." Nefaria threw the arrowheads back with astonishing force, but Clint dodged to avoid them. He was already reloading when something slammed into him from the side.

Mandrill bared his fangs and made a series of hoarse, panting hoots. Clint didn't need to speak baboon to know he'd just been threatened.

"Mandrill, get your monkey breath out of my face." Clint flipped the mutant onto his back, then used his bow to block a powerful roundhouse kick. *Crap. No sign of Nefaria.*

"Without your bow, you are just a puny little man," said Mandrill, yanking the recurve from Clint's hands with inhuman strength. As if smelling weakness, three more inmates crowded in: One had a face like a patchwork corpse, and the other two were just blurs in Clint's peripheral vision.

"At least I don't have a big red ass face." Clint yanked the belt out of his pants loops and whipped it, buckle side up, in a quick arc. The buckle opened up a cut on Mandrill's cheek, close to his right eye. He dropped Clint's bow and ran.

While Clint dealt with the other three goons, he spotted Natasha grappling with Foolkiller and Cutthroat. Foolkiller grabbed her arms, holding her captive as Cutthroat drew back his hand to strike her. Kicking up, Natasha sent her attacker flying before head-butting the man behind her.

"She's holding her own," said Luke, who was pummeling Carnage. "That's some girl you got there."

"She's not my girl," said Clint. *In fact, I might have to kill her.*

"How about I stripe up your ugly hide?" hissed Carnage. His tendrils had taken on the shape of whips, which he lashed across Luke's massive shoulders and back.

"Sorry, Cletus. Unbreakable skin."

"Then I'm going to stick my tendril in your ear and squeeze."

"Now, that's just plain nasty," said Luke, smashing Carnage against the wall. "Jess? You need some help?"

"Nah, I got this one," said Jessica, snapping handcuffs on a man with a tattoo of a mermaid on his bicep.

"Miss? I'm afraid that's not completely accurate," said the man.

"Aw, crap," said Luke. "Jess, that's Morrie Bench!"

Jessica furrowed her brow. "There's an arch-criminal down here named Morrie?"

"You can, of course, call me Hydro-Man," said Morrie, his hands dissolving into water.

"Cleanup in aisle three," said Clint, reclaiming his bow. He had a chemical neutralizer in one of his tips that could reverse Morrie's change, but there was no time left to get the arrow nocked and ready. Morrie Bench had become a man-shaped liquid, and then he began to gush forward, suddenly gaining in volume.

"Hold your breath!" Clint grabbed for Natasha's belt just as the powerful rush of water knocked everyone off their feet. Within moments, the corridor was submerged. Clint tried to swim with the fierce current, alert for a way out of this situation. He locked eyes with Natasha for a moment; to his relief, she looked completely focused and calm. *Of course she does, idiot. She's the Black Widow.*

Just as Clint was about to run out of options as well as air, he saw Luke Cage smashing through a door. Clint swam for it, Natasha by his side. A ramp led upward, and the water subsided.

Clint spent a moment on all fours, choking a little, before he could look up and take in his surroundings properly. They were in another hallway, one with a great big hole in the ceiling. A group of inmates was huddled together, apparently taking turns punching and kicking some unfortunate soul.

"Oh, God, hope that's not a guard," said Jessica, coughing up water.

"Hey," yelled the unfortunate soul. "A little help here?"

Clint, Jessica, Luke and Natasha waded in, peeling

off bad guys and disabling them in a surprisingly efficient team effort. One of the men held up his hands as Clint was about to strike him.

"Stop! I'm a medical doctor. I was not part of this mob, believe me. If you want, I will look at your friend's injuries." The man had an unusual accent—Greek? Romanian? Something in his face made Clint hesitate.

"Just give me your hands." Clint handcuffed the guy with a bolo and turned his attention back to the fight. The tide had turned, and now Clint could see the young man who had been at the bottom of the pile. This wasn't another inmate, Clint realized. Even though his left eye was swollen shut and his nose was streaming blood, the red-and-blue web-patterned costume was unmistakable.

Luke helped him up. "You lost your mask, kid."

"Don't worry," said Spider-Man, pausing to spit out a mouthful of blood. "Nobody's going to recognize me for at least a week. Oh, hell, my head's tingling again—hey, you, look out!"

Clint turned to see a monster bearing down on him. From the waist up, it was a squat, burly man with a head of writhing snakes; from the waist down, it was a gigantic, scuttling spider. Clint selected an arrow and reached for his bow. It wasn't there. *Damn it, the current.*

Just as the man-snake-spider thing reared up on its back two arachnid legs, a metal disc came spinning through the air, knocking the monster down. As Clint watched, the shield—with its distinctive red-white-and-blue stars-and-stripes pattern—sailed back up through the hole in the ceiling. Captain America emerged in the next second, his shield strapped over his arm.

Wish I could get my bow to do that, thought Clint.

Captain America managed to radiate confidence, even with his costume burnt and shredded. "Sorry it took me so long to get down here," he told Spider-Man.

"What, didn't I look like I had it all under control?" Despite his attempt to sound casual, Spider-Man's face was badly bruised. He sucked in a sharp breath as he wrapped a length of webbing around his left wrist, bandaging it.

The lights overhead flickered and dimmed, then brightened. Barely legible in the unsteady light, a sign over the door reminded guards to secure each section before opening the next.

"Clint, look." Jessica pointed to two dead guards, lying facedown in the shallow water.

"I was wondering where all the guards were," said Luke, shaking his head. "Guess a lot of them wound up like those guys."

"All right," said Captain America, at the same time as Jessica. They looked at each other, and then Captain America continued. "First thing we need to do is figure out who we've got running around here. I took out maybe a dozen on my way down here, so that leaves about seventy-five, minus however many you folks managed to capture." He paused. There was an uncomfortable silence.

"Okay, so let's assume seventy-five bad guys are still on the lam."

"You really do need to get with the times, Captain," said a woman's voice from the doorway. The speaker, dressed in a white T-shirt and jeans like the male inmates, looked like a vampire: chalk-white skin, widow's peak, fanged smile, long, dangerous-looking fingernails. "Not all of us are guys, you know." Behind her, some other female inmates snickered. "Now, let me see, which manpig shall I disembowel first?"

The hooting baboon sound of Mandrill's battle cry preceded him as he swung into the room. He paused, a look of almost comic astonishment on his face.

"Nekra?"

The vampire woman took a step forward. "Jerome?"

In the blink of an eye, the two were entwined in an intimate, mouth-devouring embrace.

"You know, I really hope they don't plan on having children," said Clint, ducking as a massive, troll-like female inmate took a swing at his head.

"Attraction isn't all about looks," said Jessica, as she faced off against a skinny blonde with red-rimmed eyes.

"Watch out for that one," said Captain America, blocking a blow from a strapping inmate who had to be over six-foot-five. "That's Toxic Doxie. Don't let her bleed on you."

"You ask me, the women here are worse than the

men," said Luke. He swept his leg under Poundcake, who had been stamping on the floor and causing the stones to shake.

"Do you really think so, Cage?" Killgrave, the Purple Man, was flanked by six other male inmates as he walked toward Luke; but the real danger was Killgrave himself, no longer looking drugged and helpless. "I think you're wrong. In fact, I think you're so wrong that I suggest you kill all your friends—and then yourself."

"Kill...all...my...friends?" Luke's eyes had a strange, faraway look.

"Oh, this is just too delicious for words. I think this is even sweeter than when I convinced your wife to kneel down and worship me." Killgrave made a little kissy face.

Luke was still facing Clint. As Clint ran through the best strategy for fighting an opponent with superior strength and unbreakable skin, he felt Natasha press something into his hands: his bow. She must have found it on the floor. And she'd given it back to him.

Clint knew better than to read too much into this— hell, they were surrounded, and the bow might not have been her weapon of choice—but still, he felt a twinge of unease. It was hard enough to kill someone at close range, let alone someone who had stood shoulder to shoulder with you in battle.

He couldn't think about that now. He had to stay focused, watch Luke's eyes, figure out Luke's first move before he made it.

"Killgrave." Cage's voice sounded thick, almost drugged. "Your...powers."

"What about them?"

"They didn't come back yet." As he spoke, Luke turned and slammed the heel of his right hand into Killgrave's face. After that, he punctuated each blow with a different curse. Clint caught a word here and there: "wife" and "child" and "hard to say 'uncle' without any teeth," followed by a few more choice expletives.

"I thought Luke only ever said 'Sweet Christmas,'" said Spider-Man, tying up the last of the female inmates with his webbing.

"His wife's trying to get him to stop cursing. Guess he's going to owe some quarters to the swear jar," said Jessica.

After a few moments, Purple Man went limp. Clint and Captain America pulled Luke off. "Easy, Luke," Cap said.

"On the bright side," said Natasha, "now we only have seventy-four to worry about." Abruptly, she moved, shoving Jessica hard against the wall.

"What the—"

"On the ceiling!" Natasha pointed to Carnage's red, alien form, slithering back toward them.

Jesssica tried to fire her gun, but nothing happened. *She must be out of bullets,* thought Clint. He shot three arrows at Carnage's head. One arrow stuck in Carnage's eye, and the other two went straight through his throat and chest, but did not appear to faze him; his muscles bunched like a cat's.

As Clint fired an exploding arrow at the creature, Jessica tossed her gun aside and threw up her hands, as if she still could fire bio-electric blasts. "Nothing's working!" She sounded furious, which meant she was frightened. "Who knows how to deal with this thing?"

"That would be me." Spider-Man extended his wrists, and jets of webbing shot out, encasing Carnage in a makeshift cocoon. Carnage struggled, but the webbing held him fast. "That'll stop him, but not for long."

Natasha blew a strand of hair out of her face. "What is that thing?"

Spider-Man looked at her. "Spongy alien symbiote outside, creamy sociopath filling. Who are you?"

"She's not one of us," said Jessica.

"She's not with them."

"She's a prisoner in our custody," said Clint, "but right now, she's working with us."

"And we need all the help we can get," said Captain America.

"Poor little super heroes." Carnage was scrabbling at the cocoon of webbing that held him, causing odd pockets to bulge out. "Most of us are probably near the surface level by now. You can't win this one."

"Hey," said Luke, cautiously peering into a shadowy corner. "Anyone see Baboon Boy and Vampire Girl? Either they went to find a room, or they're headed for a night on the town."

Inside his cocoon, Carnage giggled. "You're lo-sing!"

Peter flicked his wrist and added another layer of webbing, muffling Carnage's words. "What was that? Couldn't make it out."

"He's right, though," said Captain America. "This

is spiraling out of control. We need to get back up to the surface and stop anyone else from escaping."

"Good idea," said Jessica, trying one of the doors. It led to a corridor lined with more doors. "We're too far underground to get any cell-phone reception here, but I think we might get a signal if we could climb back up to B level."

"Over here," said Clint. He yanked hard at a doorknob, but it didn't give. "Something's jamming it."

"Hang on a sec," said Luke. He yanked the door off its hinges, revealing the chair that had been shoved up against it. The fire stairs had been painted gunmetal gray and smelled of dust and cigarette smoke; clearly, they were only used by guards sneaking an unofficial cigarette break.

"Okay," said Captain America. "Let's go!"

Their footsteps were loud on the stone and metal stairs, and no one attempted to talk. They had entered the stairwell at the eighth and bottom level; on the fourth level, they found a dead guard—his brown eyes opened wide in shock, an enormous, gaping wound in his chest.

"No weapon," said Clint, checking the man's body. His hands came away stained with blood.

"We've got to keep moving," said Captain America.

Clint wiped his hands on his pants, and then closed the dead guard's eyes before following the others. Natasha, just ahead of him, looked back at him. "We haven't seen any other guards besides the two dead ones and this one."

"I know. And there are supposed to be sixty-seven S.H.I.E.L.D. agents stationed here."

"Maybe they're being held as hostages."

"Maybe."

Natasha stopped moving, one foot raised on the next step.

"This is it," Captain America called back down the stairs. "Step back while I open this door. We don't know what we're going up against, so brace yourselves."

The door crashed open, and they found themselves standing directly below the demolished roof. There were at least eighty bodies crammed into the remains of the lobby—all of them busily shouting and jostling, and passing around guns and combat vests and laptops looted from the prison. Rain sleeted down, making the scene even more surreal. A low animal growl rose from the crowd.

"Guess we found everyone," said Peter.

"Captain," said a voice with a honeyed Italian accent, "Are you here to deliver a blistering lecture on our moral shortcomings?"

"No. I'm here to put you down."

"How amusing." Nefaria gave a conjurer's wave of his hand, and then there were *ten* Nefarias, each laughing with impossibly white teeth. The mob behind him let out a roar and attacked.

Clint felt a blow to his head, whirled and aimed a kick at a cloaked figure who dissolved—leaving him off balance and vulnerable to an attack from an orange, armor-plated tank of a man.

As Clint aimed an arrow at the Armadillo, he realized some of the figures he saw coming at him were actually holographic projections. When he looked out of the corner of his eyes at them, the illusions wavered. "Luke," he shouted, trying to warn him. But to his shock, Luke turned and slammed his fist into Clint's stomach.

"What the—"

As Luke lunged for him again, Clint saw that the big man's eyes had turned opaque and milky. In the corner of the room, Clint spotted Purple Man smiling, his face still bloody from Luke's earlier beating.

Guess he got his powers back.

"Luke!" Captain America caught Cage's fist. "You have to fight whatever's—" Heavy hands grabbed Captain America under the jaw, cutting him off midsentence. With a gigantic heave, Crusher Creel tossed Captain America up and out of the gaping hole in the roof.

"Captain!" Jessica struggled in Creel's thickly muscled embrace.

"What do you have for me, little girl?" asked Creel, squeezing the breath out of Jessica. "Is there something worth absorbing?" As Jessica sagged, beginning to pass out, Creel grunted. "No, how disappointing. Nothing but a weak human female. Kindest to just break your neck and…hang on." The man's bald head came up, as if he'd been struck. "Well, what do you know? There *is* a—"

Jessica's hand shot out, and she poked two stiffened fingers into Creel's eyes. Howling, he hunched over, clutching his face. Jessica kicked him in the back, toppling him.

At the same time this was happening, Captain America flipped himself in midair. But it was no use—there was no way for him to break his fall, nothing for him to grab on to.

"Cap!" Spider-Man shot a jet of webbing from his unbroken wrist, but it didn't extend far enough. Just as Captain America began plummeting down, a flash of metallic red and gold shot through the sky.

"Can't leave you kids alone for a minute," said Iron Man, grabbing Captain America under the armpits. "What happened down there?"

"You got me. I was on my way to a security conference in Washington."

Down below, a dozen inmates had left the brawl and were climbing up out of the roof. A few had already made it onto the landing dock where the S.H.I.E.L.D. agents stood like zombies, their milk-pale eyes glazed over—more victims of Killgrave's hypnotic power.

Iron Man swooped down, releasing Captain America a few feet from the ground. "Maybe we were a bit hasty breaking up the Avengers," he said, aiming a blast from the palms of his metal gauntlets down at the ground and trapping two of the inmates in a barricade of fire.

"We didn't break up," said Captain America, punching an inmate before he could slice open a guard's throat with razor-sharp claws. "You broke us up."

"I may have said the words," said Iron Man, "but I think we both knew the thrill was gone."

"Guys," said Clint. "A little more focus on the here and now?" He aimed a Vibranium-tipped arrow at Carnage, who had escaped his webbed cocoon and was now gleefully tangling Spider-Man in his barbed tendrils. The arrow passed straight through Carnage, leaving a hole that closed up even as Clint watched.

"You trying to say you need a little help?" Tony directed a fusillade of fiery blasts at Carnage.

Clint turned just in time to see Luke rounding on Natasha, who had been using his powerful body as a shield. Natasha flicked her wrist, sending a circular blade whizzing through the air. It passed scant centimeters from Luke's nose, arcing across the room and hitting Purple Man squarely in the forehead.

As the violet-skinned telepath fell unconscious, Luke released Natasha. Caught off balance, Natasha began to fall into the path of Iron Man's chest-mounted Uni-beam.

Without thinking, Clint threw himself on top of Natasha and knocked her to the side. Searing heat passed over his back; he was going to have a burn. "You okay?"

Natasha looked up at him with a little half-smile playing around her mouth. "Sure. Do you always do this at the end of a fight?"

He wondered how much she could feel through the Vibranium body armor. "What makes you think it's the end?"

"Your friend over there."

Clint moved his body off Natasha so she could breathe, and there was Iron Man, demolishing their opponents like a futuristic red-and-gold knight.

"Hey, guys. Want to come back to my house when we're all done?" His voice came out of the helmet sounding a little brassy.

Captain America nailed Jigsaw with one blow to his misaligned face. "Only if you don't order pizza again." All around them, inmates were slowing down, stopping, looking. Clint felt himself grinning and turned back to Nat.

For the first time all evening, she wasn't at his side.

Damn it. Clint selected the arrow from his quiver and nocked it as he scanned the room. In the midst of all the writhing, fighting bodies, some human and some scaled or winged or furred, Clint went very still. He spotted her walking almost calmly through the chaos of battle, as if she trusted her confidence alone to keep her unharmed.

Sighting down the arrow, Clint made an adjustment. Jessica kicked a villain in front of the Black Widow, forcing Natasha to hesitate. As if she felt the weight of Clint's gaze, Natasha turned; for a moment, she looked back at him, just as she had back on the Helicarrier. This time, there was no mocking come-hither smile. Instead, Natasha faced him fully, making herself an easier target.

Because of her Vibranium armor, of course, he would have to go for a head shot. Clint wondered what Nat would have done if she had known there were no more ingenious Stark Industries arrows left in his quiver. He would have to choose: kill her, or let her escape. Except there was no choice. He was a S.H.I.E.L.D. agent, and he had his orders: *If at any point you think Romanova poses any kind of a threat, or if she shows any signs of attempting to escape, neutralize her.*

He even had the Widow's permission. *If I'm not going to walk out of here, kill me. That's why she's waiting for me to make up my mind,* Clint realized. *She's giving me the choice.*

Slowly, carefully, he lowered his bow. Natasha did smile then, a smile that seemed as rueful as the thoughts racing through his head. He was going to pay for this, he knew.

Then she was gone, and someone was jumping on him, and there was no more time for reflection.

The next half hour was a blur of activity as Iron Man helped Captain America and the S.H.I.E.L.D. agents round up forty-four of the inmates.

As he was leaving, Clint spotted a circular blade marked with a small black-and-red symbol wedged into the wall. A black widow spider.

Clint slipped the blade into an outside pocket in his vest. He figured he might as well keep a souvenir of the brief relationship that had probably just ended his career.

SIX

DESPITE her fatigue, Jessica Drew stood at attention in Commander Hill's office—spine straight, arms at her sides and feet at a regulation forty-five-degree angle with the heels together. She could smell the hot, slightly bitter coffee sitting on Hill's desk. It was five in the morning, and Jessica was tired and sore, but still pumped up from the long night of fighting. She could have used a cup of coffee, too, and a doughnut, either powdered sugar or sugar glazed. Possibly both.

"I know Director Fury thought highly of you, Agent Drew. But Fury's not here right now. And I, for one, am not overly impressed with your performance to date." Hill didn't say any more about Nick Fury's whereabouts, and Jessica wondered whether the other woman knew as much about the details of his mission as she herself did. Probably not.

"I am aware that until fairly recently, you had powers to fall back on. This does not, in my opinion, excuse your part in what amounts to total assignment failure."

"No, ma'am," Jessica replied automatically, even though she thought this grossly unfair. No wonder Hill was so disliked. Unlike Fury, who faced up to unpleasant truths, Hill tended to massage the facts to suit her plans. She was also a poor manager of people. The only reason she could have had to remind Jessica about the loss of her powers was to throw her off balance. But there was no underlying strategy here as far as Jessica could tell.

Fury, on the other hand, never did anything without a solid and specific reason.

"All of this forces me to reevaluate your role within S.H.I.E.L.D.," Hill went on, and then paused. She seemed to be waiting for some sort of a response; Jessica nodded.

The truth was, Jessica was only half-listening to the litany of her failings. In the midst of the battle last night, she had felt the first real tingle of her old powers returning. Until that moment, she had been convinced the operation had been a failure, and that Hydra had either lied to her about having the technology to restore her powers or been mistaken in their capabilities. But when she had attempted to fire her gun into the alien symbiote and discovered she was out of bullets, the surge of adrenaline must have triggered something.

Hydra might be an organization of ruthless international terrorists, but they had kept their side of the bargain. Jessica just hoped she hadn't slipped up last night when she had aimed her bio-electric blasts at Carnage. In all the confusion, she didn't think anyone had noticed her using her powers, but it was hard to tell with Clint and Luke—they tended to keep to themselves. Still, she didn't think they'd twigged to her mistake. Luke had been rattled by the Purple Man, and Clint—well, he had been too distracted by the Black Widow to notice anything. *Wonder what would have happened if I had* all *my powers back.*

The injected DNA of a radioactive spider had given Jessica many of the same abilities as Peter Parker: heightened agility and speed, the ability to stick to walls, and a highly intuitive sense of impending danger. The experimental treatments Jessica's father had given her had also imbued her with abilities Spider-Man did not possess: the ability to shoot bio-electric blasts from her hands, and a natural, pheromone-based scent that attracted heterosexual men—and repelled heterosexual women. Jessica wasn't entirely sure she wanted that part of her power to return. It was a relief to sit next to a man you liked and not have to remember to keep your defenses tamped down. And how lovely to get to know a man and discover whether he was really attracted to you as a person, rather than just compelled by your screwy body chemistry.

Of course, the flip side of being normal was discovering that the man you liked only regarded you as a friend. *Perhaps that Black Widow person had some interesting pheromones of her own.* Jessica, for one, had felt dislike at first sight for the Russian. But then, that might have had something to do with watching her ordinarily imperturbable partner leaving himself wide open to attack.

Something in Commander Hill's voice suggested she was finally getting to the point. Jessica focused on Fury's replacement, trying to keep all expression from her face.

"And so, Agent Drew, I'm having both you and Agent Barton pulled from all active-duty assignments. Unlike Barton, you will not be investigated for dereliction of duty, but you will be expected to cooperate in the investigation."

"I don't see why you have to investigate Clint, Commander Hill. After all, there's no way he could have anticipated the breakout." *And you're the genius who put him in charge of the Widow,* Jessica added silently.

Hill's lips thinned. "If that is the case, then that is what the investigation will reveal." Her phone chimed; she glanced down at it for a moment, and then texted back. When she was done, she said, "Oh, by the way, since you'll be doing purely support work, you should change out of uniform."

"All right," said Jessica. "Am I dismissed?"

"Of course," said Hill. Jessica waited. No point in heading for the door. Hill would just call her back at the last minute. She had read about this technique in a World War II novel. *Of course you can go home, Mademoiselle. Ah, but there is one more thing: First give us the name of your contact in the Resistance.*

Hill looked annoyed as she realized Jessica wasn't falling for the trick. "Oh, well, there is one more thing."

Jessica met Maria Hill's cold blue gaze and knew it

was going to be worse than she had expected. "Yes?"

"You've been reassigned. You're not working with Agent Barton anymore."

JESSICA walked back to her old desk to gather her things and saw Clint, wearing one of Coulson's old, ill-fitting suits. He looked adorably stoic, but Jessica, who knew him well, could tell he would probably have preferred a court martial to this demotion.

"So you get to keep doing active work?" He smiled, and it was genuine. "Good for you. I'm supposed to go sit next to Coulson to learn spreadsheets."

Jessica looked down at her black jumpsuit. "Oh, this. No, I've been moved, too. I just haven't had time to shower and change out of uniform yet."

"Oh, hell. Jess, I'm sorry."

"Hawkeye," said Jessica. He looked up, and the look in his eyes killed the joke she was about to make. She held out her hand. "Come on."

"Jessica, there's no point trying to talk Commander Hill out of this."

"That's not where we're going." Since he didn't take her hand, she grabbed him by the sleeve and pulled him up.

"What's the plan? Jump off the ship in protest?"

"Like you'd leave your bow behind."

"It's not really my bow, as Commander Hill reminded me."

"Right. Like they didn't use your input in designing it. Like anyone else could use it." They emerged onto the deck of the Helicarrier. Suddenly, Jessica felt she could breathe again. The air was cool and brisk, and had that indefinable late-autumn smell. Behind them, the sun was rising in a blaze of gold and amber and rose, the ruddy colors making the dark spires and towers of Lower Manhattan appear like something out of a fairy tale. Below them, the Statue of Liberty came into sight—first a dark silhouette, and then bathed in early morning sunlight that lightened the oxidized green of her outstretched copper arm.

"Emma Lazarus called her the mother of exiles," said Jessica.

"How do you know that? You didn't even grow up in the U.S., right?"

"There's a course you take when you become a citizen."

Jessica had been raised in Transia, a tiny East European country, but both her parents had been British nationals. After her father's experiments in accelerating evolution had gone awry, though, she had been raised by Lady Bova—a lovely, compassionate woman who had once been a Jersey cow.

"You probably know more about American history than I do, then," said Clint.

Jessica's hair blew into her face, and she tucked it back. "There's no probably about it."

"Hey there," said a familiar voice, and a square-jawed blond man came toward them. "I tell you, this is one view that hasn't changed too much." He was wearing a black T-shirt and jeans, but carried himself like a military man. It took Jessica a moment to recognize him.

"I don't suppose you got in trouble, did you, Captain?"

"Call me Steve, please. And don't tell me you two caught flak? After we put forty-five of the Raft inmates back in their cells?"

"We've been turned into suits," said Jessica. "Clint's going to be investigated."

"Ah. I thought I saw your bow in the armory when I locked up my shield." Steve Rogers put his thumbs in his pockets and looked thoughtful. "Seems a heck of a shame."

A sudden gust of hot wind made Jessica shield her face. She looked up to see Tony Stark blasting down in his red-and-gold Iron Man suit, faceplate raised. "I just made a quick run to H&H," he said, indicating the brown paper bag in his hands. "Who wants coffee and who wants a bagel?"

There was something a little incongruous about seeing Tony's lean, slightly shopworn face with its shrewd brown eyes and diabolical goatee emerging from the gleaming, articulated armor. Up close, there were no outward signs of the man's struggles with alcohol or the heart problems that had inspired him to create the miniature arc reactor he wore in his chest. The reactor kept shrapnel from entering his heart and fueled the Iron Man armor—a pretty nifty trick, especially considering the fact that Tony had invented the gizmo while being held prisoner by terrorists.

Jessica took a bagel and a cup of coffee. "What kind

of cream cheese is this?"

"I don't know, maybe scallion. Here, I think this one's plain."

"You've already taken a bite out of it!"

"And you've got some weird slime on your sleeve. Didn't you take a shower yet?"

"Nope. I probably don't get as sweaty as you do in that suit."

"My suit's air-conditioned." Tony turned to Clint, offering him the bagel bag. "What about you, Katniss?"

"You want to know if I showered? Smell me."

"No breakfast for you, wiseass." He turned to Steve. "Cap?"

"Thanks."

While Tony's back was turned, Jessica offered Clint her bagel. He shook his head and showed her that he had already acquired one. For a moment, there was silence as everyone chewed and contemplated the sunrise.

"So," said Steve, "that was some day we had, yesterday."

"Forty-two still at large," said Tony, pulling off an iron gauntlet so he could eat a bagel.

"Forty-three," said Clint. "If you include the Black Widow."

Tony nodded. "I'll add her to my database. I'm still figuring out who was behind it. Probably Nefaria or Electro or one of the other electrical guys."

"I thought Electro had gone straight and was working a real job," said Steve.

Jessica took a big gulp of coffee, burning her

tongue. "He could have broken into the Raft. But Max Dillon's not smart enough to mastermind an escape from a locked bathroom stall."

"So who could have hired him?" Steve frowned, thinking. "Nefaria? Someone on the inside?"

Tony brushed a crumb off his beard. "I'll question the prisoners back at the Raft. One of them has to know something."

Jessica, Clint and Steve exchanged glances. "Or I could do it," said Jessica. "Oh, crud, I forgot. I've been put on desk duty." Her heart was pounding, because she could tell this wasn't just a casual conversation anymore. Steve was putting something together, here. "I can't believe the bad guys are getting away, and we don't get to play any part in bringing them back in."

Steve looked at her, not saying anything, then looked out at the lightening sky.

Jessica pretended to watch the horizon, as well—no longer tired, but trying to keep from giving the game away by appearing too eager. *Let him make the offer,* she thought. *Don't push too hard.*

"You know, we were good back there," said Steve. "We worked together like a team."

"Tell that to Commander Hill," said Clint.

"I already did. I also told her that last night reminded me of the early days of the Avengers."

"You mean, before the Scarlet Witch went psycho and decided that reality needed a makeover?" Tony took another bite of his bagel. "Yeah, it was all fine and dandy before everything went to hell."

"Last night's job isn't done yet," said Steve, stretching out his arms on the railing. "There are still a lot of dangerous criminals out there."

"Like I told you, I'm working on it," said Tony.

"Don't think it's a one-man job. Not even a lot of one-man jobs. This is going to take a team effort, Tony."

To everyone's surprise, Tony gave a bark of laughter. "Aw, jeez, don't tell me you're talking about reassembling the Avengers?"

"Tony, if you'll just give me a chance to explain…"

"What about the little fact that I just don't have the money to fund the team anymore, huh? My little misunderstanding with the Latverian ambassador didn't exactly help my cred."

Jessica and Clint exchanged glances. Like everyone else, they had heard about the events leading up to the Avengers' breakup on the news. But this was an insiders' fight.

"Tony, if you'll just shut up long enough for me to get a word in edgewise, you'd understand that I'm not talking about assembling the same team. I'm talking about a new team. The team we were working with last night."

"Oh." Tony took a sip of coffee. "I'm still not paying for it, though."

"No one said you have to pay for it."

"Commander Hill is never going to approve this," said Jessica. "She doesn't like to cede power to anyone."

Steve smiled, and for a moment Jessica felt as though she were in an old World War II movie. The only thing missing was that little swell of background music. Steve said, "Actually, I've already gotten permission from Washington to assemble a task force. We don't need Hill's permission."

Jessica couldn't keep herself from grinning. "So where are we going to have the secret clubhouse, Steve?" It still felt strange, calling him by his first name.

"Well…" Steve looked at Tony.

Tony sighed. "I suppose you want to meet at my place."

"That would be swell, Tony."

Jessica, about to take another bite of her bagel, paused. "Are we talking about me having to wear a skintight, bright-red-and-yellow suit again?"

"I think we need to be both public and visible, yes."

Jessica threw the remainder of her bagel back into the bag. "All right, then. No more carbs for me."

Steve turned to Clint. "How about you? You in?"

Clint raised his eyebrows. "Let me get this straight. You're inviting me to join a team of super heroes."

"That's one way of looking at it."

"Why me?"

Steve looked surprised. "Are you kidding?"

"I'm good with the bow, and I can fight, but you've got people who can fly or lift school buses or fire energy bolts out of their hands. And I'm not being modest when I say I'm not exactly a scientific genius, either," he added, nodding at Tony.

"You had some good suggestions for the arrowheads," Tony offered. "And wasn't that your idea for the bow to open and close with a flick of the wrist?"

"Yeah, but I wouldn't have known how the hell to make it."

"We can't all be multi-talented," said Tony. "If I only wanted people with my level of intelligence on a team, I'd be pretty limited. I mean, Bruce Banner, maybe, and Reed Richards, and that X-Man with all the fur..."

"We don't all have powers," said Jessica, breaking in. "I don't. Just fighting skills and know-how."

"It all depends on the situation," said Steve. "Some of the most brilliant and resourceful Resistance fighters I knew were teenage girls who could take apart a Sten gun and hide it quicker than most girls today can put on their makeup."

"Yeah," said Clint. "But if you'd had a choice between a regular teenager and one with special laser fingers, I'm guessing you would have chosen the one who could singe off Hitler's moustache without the Sten gun."

"I've seen you fight, Hawkeye," said Steve, very simply. For a moment, that seemed to be his entire closing argument, but then he added, "Back in the war, I would have put you on my team. I would have known that I could send you out with nothing but the bow and a few arrows, and you'd come back. A platoon of other guys could be armed to the teeth, and I'd never see them again." Steve paused, and the rising sun burnished the gold of his hair. "People talk about super-powers. But some guys—some gals—they have something. It may not be obvious, like being able to blast energy from your fingertips. It may not even have a name. But it's real. You've got that something. That girl you were with last night— the redhead—she had it, too. Otherwise, how could she get away?"

Clint met the other man's gaze. "Don't play games with me, Cap. You know how."

"Clint, what are you saying?" Jessica stared at him, trying to understand how one admittedly pretty red-head could have undermined his loyalty in just one night. And even though she had no right, she felt betrayed.

"She saved your life. I saw it. I'm not blaming you," said Steve.

Oh, so she saved his life, thought Jessica. That made sense, then. *He felt he owed her a debt.*

Clint looked at Tony. "What's your say on this?"

Tony looked amused. "Hey, I don't care if you get killed trying to play with the big boys. Last time around, we had nothing but super-powered folks, and one of them lost her nut. You're not mentally unstable, are you?"

Clint shook his head.

"No big unresolved childhood issues? No, never mind that. I think it probably goes without saying that we all have those. Anyway, it's fine with me."

"Guess it beats doing paperwork," said Clint. "Just one thing, though."

"Name it," said Steve.

One side of Clint's mouth quirked up. "I'm not

wearing some crayon-colored onesie."

Jessica gave a whoop of laughter that frightened a pigeon from the railing.

SEVEN

THE middle-aged butler who opened the door to Tony Stark's penthouse was dressed in the traditional English morning dress of tails, bowtie, vest and striped trousers. To his credit, the butler didn't blink when he saw that Jessica was wearing a gray sweat suit and carrying a large brown paper bag. "Jessica Drew, I presume?"

"You presume correctly."

"The others are inside. Just go down the hallway." As he closed the door behind her, Jessica noticed a floating staircase wrapped around a glass elevator.

"This place takes up two floors?"

"Three," said the butler, giving her an encouraging nod.

Jessica made her way down a long, hardwood-floor hallway with brick walls. A painting of a gold android with a melting clock in her abdomen—probably an original Dali—hung on one wall, alongside a human skull encased in diamonds that had been on display at the Tate Gallery in London, until very recently.

Maybe I shouldn't have come straight from the gym, thought Jessica. It was too late to head home to change, though, because now she could see Tony, Peter, Steve and Luke, all seated on leather couches and chairs arranged beside an enormous glass wall that led out onto a wraparound balcony.

The men were all dressed for action. Steve was wearing his Captain America suit under jeans and a light leather jacket. Tony had on his Iron Man armor without the helmet, and Peter was in complete Spider-Man costume, including mask. Only Luke Cage wore regular clothes: a black turtleneck, cargo pants and rugged leather boots.

Guess Tony doesn't walk around in his underwear much. On the other hand, she thought, the billionaire inventor didn't seem like the kind of guy to give a damn about anyone else's opinion.

Hell. Jessica had been so sure this was a sweats-and-beer kind of meeting. *Sometimes it's so hard to fit in with the guys.*

"Hey, everyone," she said. "Sorry I look like this, I came straight from the gym. I brought beer, though." She pulled the six pack of Corona Light out of the paper bag. "Anyone want some?"

"Sorry," said Tony, "there's no drinking alcohol tonight. Help yourself to water, seltzer or soda, though." He pointed to a tray on a side table that looked like a giant stone head.

"Oh," said Jessica. "Sure. Um, what should I do with these?" She held out the beers.

"I'll just take those to the kitchen," said the butler.

Behind Tony's back, Steve shook his head. Clearly, this was a sensitive subject.

"Sorry," Jessica mouthed back.

"Steve," said Tony, without turning around, "stop telling the new girl that I'm a lush. Jessica, the reason I'm not serving spirits is because I was hoping to get some field work accomplished tonight."

"Before you go volunteering me for the dance committee, remember I haven't signed up yet," said Peter, sitting down on the couch. He was moving a bit stiffly, and Jessica wondered just how badly he'd been beaten last night. There was a wrist brace on his left hand, attached with Velcro straps.

"Aren't you going to take your mask off?"

Peter pulled the fabric up so his nose and mouth were uncovered and took a sip of water. "I like to preserve a sense of mystery."

"What do you think they're going to do, post your picture on Facebook?"

"Unlike some people, Ms. Drew, I actually have a secret identity."

"Everyone here and at least two dozen Raftees saw you without your mask last night. You do remember that, right?"

Peter tugged his mask back down over his chin. "I *remember* telling you it was all right to call yourself Spider-Woman. Now I take it back."

"Hang on a minute," said Luke, taking a handful of almonds from a silver bowl. "I just realized. Spider-Man, Spider-Woman—you guys related, or what?"

"Yes," said Jessica, tugging at Peter's mask. "He's my brother."

"No, I am not," said Peter. "And would you mind not doing that?"

"You're injured, aren't you? That's what you're hiding."

"No, really, what's the deal with you two?" Luke pointed at Peter. "Boyfriend and girlfriend?"

"Are you kidding? He's getting married. Or got married," said Jessica, wondering where Clint was. "Also, he's *like* my brother."

This was not exactly true. Jessica had met Peter back when she was new to New York. Nick Fury had just recruited her, but he wasn't around much, and Jessica was missing her old friends at Hydra. She couldn't really go back, of course, not after learning the organization was responsible for terrorist activities all over the globe, but Hydra had been more than just a job. It had been like a family. Suddenly she was on her own most of the time, making headlines as Spider-Woman, but eating dinner alone in her apartment while watching CNN.

That had changed when Jessica met Spider-Man on patrol one night, and learned they had more in common than just their professional names. Peter had taught her a great deal about how to use her powers, and she found herself crushing on him for a good long time. Part of the appeal had been that back when she had her full powers, Pete and Nick Fury had been the only two men who were completely immune to her pheromonal charisma. Jessica had viewed Fury as a mentor, but she had always wondered whether Pete would have found her attractive if he hadn't been with Mary Jane. No point thinking about that now, of course, since he and MJ were probably in full honeymoon mode.

"Actually," said Peter, "Mary Jane and I just broke up."

"Oh," said Jessica. As she tried to think of something to say, Clint came in from the balcony, dressed for action in a black vest and combat pants, a partial gauntlet on his left arm.

"Hey, Jess. That's some view," he said to Tony. "And some plane you've got on the roof. What is it, some new experimental prototype? It kind of looks like an updated SR-71 Blackbird."

"It's nothing like the Blackbird," said Tony, visibly annoyed. "And that was supposed to be a surprise. How did you get on the roof from here, anyhow? You don't fly."

"I thought it looked like a Blackbird, too," said Steve, joining the other two men.

"Hey, Drew" said a familiar female voice. Jessica grinned in delight as she recognized Jessica Jones, Luke Cage's wife.

"Jones, you bad girl, what have you been up to?" Jessica ran up to hug the other woman, and then hesitated, looking down at the size of Jones's pregnant belly. "It is safe to hug you, isn't it?"

"It's not catching, if that's what you mean."

"You look wonderful."

"Please. My face is all puffy. In the movies, pregnant

women never get puffy faces. And I don't know how I can be retaining fluid—I go to the bathroom every other minute. You should check out the restrooms here, though—the toilet does everything but serenade you."

Jessica laughed. It was difficult to reconcile this relaxed, smiling pregnant woman with the edgy, hard-drinking detective Jessica had known just a couple of years earlier. "When are you due?"

"She's in her eighth month," said Luke, putting his arm around his wife.

"I still think I should be part of the new team," said Jones. "I could be Preggo Woman."

Tony looked at her, frowning. "You are joking, right? Because while I have a great deal of respect for your abilities…"

"I don't know, Tony, I hear some guys are deathly afraid of pregnant women…" She approached him, and Tony held up his hands.

"I'm perfectly fine with pregnant women, as long as they keep themselves covered. By which I mean, no magazine nudity until you have your figure back."

Jessica Jones put her hands on her hips. "Tony Stark…"

Luke stood up. "Want me to beat him up for you, honey?"

Tony shook his head. "Hang on, you *want* me to see your wife naked right now?"

Steve cleared his throat. "Tony, how about we leave the subject of other men's wives and take a look at who's missing from the Raft."

"Good idea." Tony did something Jessica couldn't

see, and the picture windows went opaque as a holographic wall of faces appeared in the middle of the room. There, in a triple-tiered row, were the faces and specs on the forty-two Raft inmates still at large. "Now, I've already unearthed some recovered security-camera footage from last night, and we were right about Electro being the proximate cause of the breakout. I've done a check on money transfers. Max Dillon has withdrawn money from a Swiss account and had it wired to a bank in Boston. I ran a facial-recognition search, and Dillon's been spotted at a local restaurant." Tony grinned. "Who's up for a trip to Beantown?"

"You do know that most of us can't fly," said Luke. "What are you going to do, carry us all there in a big sack?"

"I could do that," said Tony. "Or we could take the jet that's parked on the roof."

Tony led them to the glass elevator, which brought them to the very top of the tower. The night was cool and a little windy. All around them, the city lights twinkled. From this height, Manhattan looked like a playground. To anyone with powers, the urge to jump or leap from rooftop to rooftop was almost irresistible.

"Maybe you've heard rumors about a new generation of supersonic stealth plane," said Tony. "Meet the reality." With a showman's timing, Tony pressed a button that caused two walls to fold down, revealing a sleek, futuristic black jet with a needle-sharp nose. "Who's up for a short flight to bring back Electro?"

"You don't really need all of us to bring in Max,"

said Jessica, "and I think I'd be of more use doing some data analysis." She didn't mention the fact that she didn't want to see herself on the news in gray sweats, featured under *What Not to Wear, Super-Hero Edition*.

"And I'd better take my wife home before she has to go to the bathroom again," said Luke, pressing the elevator button.

"Actually, we're going to go home and fool around," said Jones as the elevator doors closed after them.

"Didn't need to know that," said Tony, turning to Peter. "So, you game?"

Peter lifted his left arm, drawing attention to the wrist brace. "Sorry." Jessica remained on the roof with Peter. They watched together as the jet took off, moving with astonishing speed until the small, blinking lights on its wingtips disappeared over the horizon. "Hey," she said. "You want to tell me what's really going on? I've never known an injury to keep you on the sidelines before."

"I wanted to ask you a favor." He paused. "I need to get back into the Raft to question some of the inmates."

Jessica stared at him for a moment, surprised, then laughed. "Hang on, you can't mean you want me to use my S.H.I.E.L.D. influence for something. After all your lectures about the pernicious culture of compartmentalized loyalty?"

"You going to help me, or not?"

"Of course I am. I just want to get my licks in."

Peter pulled his mask off so she could see his face.

"All joking aside, Jessica, I still don't trust S.H.I.E.L.D. And neither should you."

Jessica put her hand on his cheek. "Ouch. They really worked you over. How is the rest of you?"

"Painful. I'm pretty much black and blue from crotch to sternum. But it's better when I'm moving—it's sitting still that makes everything seize up." He pulled his mask back down so the bruises and scars were hidden behind the expressionless spider-face.

"Pete. You sure you should be doing this in your condition?"

"*I'm* not pregnant."

"Very funny." Jessica looked at the other, smaller skyscrapers, so far below them they seemed like toy houses. She put her hand on his shoulder and felt him tense. "I'm just saying, be careful."

"That's the plan. You going to make that call for me?"

"Wait a minute. You're going there *now*?"

Peter shrugged. "Call me competitive, but I wouldn't mind coming up with the goods before Mister I-Have-My-Own-Jet does." Peter launched himself into the night, falling for a long while before catching himself on a web.

Jessica hoped he got to the Raft before the pain caught up with him.

JESSICA stopped in front of the nondescript Midtown building, one of several locations S.H.I.E.L.D. maintained for its Manhattan-based operatives. A retinal scan admitted her into the inner lobby, and then a guard checked her ID before allowing her into the elevator.

She punched in her personal security code and a password no one else knew, and then she was finally inside the tiny studio. She flicked on the lights.

"What took you so long?"

Jessica gasped and dropped her container of salad and soda. She went into a fighter's crouch before she saw who it was. "Jesus," she said, bending down to pick up a runaway tomato. "You made me ruin my dinner."

"Nonsense," said Nick Fury. "A little dirt won't hurt you."

Jessica looked up at the lean, battle-scarred man with the eyepatch. "Some kinds of dirt are harder to shake than others."

"I don't see the problem. It's not like you're *really* working for Hydra."

Jessica didn't try to explain that there were moments when she actually felt guilty about that. She knew Hydra was a terrorist organization, but not all the people who worked for Hydra were evil. Some of them had known her for more than a decade, remembered her birthday, teased her about liking anchovies on pizza. Since she couldn't admit any of this to Fury, Jessica just said, "It just feels wrong, keeping secrets from my teammates."

Fury sat up straighter in his chair. "So the Avengers are a team again?"

Jessica looked down at the squashed tomato in her hand. In the dim light, it looked a little like blood. "I don't know, sir. Spider-Man is hesitant, and so is Luke

Cage, because of his wife's advanced pregnancy. I think Clint Barton is in, though." He had certainly jetted off to Boston readily enough.

"And what did you tell Hydra?"

Jessica took a deep breath. "I told them it looked like it was happening." She stood up and threw out the ruined container of salad. "Was that the right thing to do?"

"Yes." Director Fury stood up and walked toward the door. Jessica noticed he was limping. "Any sign that their experimental treatment is working?"

"Yes," said Jessica. "I think it might be." She felt nervous saying it out loud, in case she jinxed something. Which was ridiculous, she knew.

"Show me." Fury pulled a quarter out of his pocket and threw it in the air.

Jessica pointed her hand and concentrated. She zapped the coin, changing its trajectory by a foot and a half. "Not very impressive," she said.

"Pretty good, actually. Fine work, Special Agent Drew. Just learning what technology their scientists have is going to be extremely useful to us."

"May I tell the others?"

"Not yet," said Fury. "I don't want Hydra realizing that you're not working with them until the last possible moment, and I suspect we may have leaks within S.H.I.E.L.D."

Jessica steeled herself to ask the question. "And if anything happens to you, sir? And the others find out that I've been dealing with Hydra?"

"No chance of that, Drew. I'm as indestructible as a cockroach."

"Wait. There's one more thing. I was actually going to call when I got home." Jessica told him about Spider-Man's request for immediate Raft access.

"Didn't want to ask Hill? I'll take care of it."

Fury left, and then Jessica was alone in the tiny apartment with its impersonal, chain-motel furniture; its serene and soulless prints of beaches and mountains; and the pervasive odor of industrial-strength detergents masquerading as violets and pine.

EIGHT

THE Liberty Café was a hotel restaurant pretending to be a bistro—as if a couple of umbrellas and brown paper table coverings could distract customers from the steel-and-glass structure surrounding it, and the $16 price tag for a hamburger and freedom fries. Clint had never paid $16 for a burger in his life and couldn't understand anyone who did, even if the patty was dolled up with homemade tomato butter and a sprig of organic parsley. Not that he was in their target demographic. The café's clientele was mainly gray-haired business folks in loafers and pumps, and hipster parents pushing the latest in stroller technology.

"And then we also have our famous Devils on Horseback," the red-haired waitress was telling her customers, "which is dates and blue cheese, wrapped in a slice of bac..." Her voice trailed off as her gaze landed on something across the lobby.

"What was that?" The fedora-wearing father looked up from his iPhone.

"Sorry. Wrapped in bacon." The waitress smiled. She had a rounded, puppyish face, accentuated by her chin-length bob.

Hipster mom clucked her tongue disapprovingly. "What was the fish special again?"

Concealed behind a barricade of potted plants and a poster-sized menu board, Clint held his arrow nocked and ready. "Is that him? The bald guy in the leather jacket?"

"That's Max," said Captain America. "The girl is Mia Matteo, an aspiring actress. She's been dating Max for about six months."

"No accounting for taste. He's making his move," said Iron Man. Down on the street, Max Dillon strode over to Mia, looking big and sinister and utterly out of place in the upscale hotel.

"Max?" Mia looked surprised and then annoyed. "What are you doing here? I thought you had a job in New York."

"Job's done. Come on." Max grabbed her elbow. "We got to go."

"Ex-cuse me," said hipster mom, "but she's got to take our order."

"Max, not now," said Mia. "You're going to get me fired."

"So what? Mia, baby, I am loaded. You don't need to deal with idiots like this anymore."

"You can't talk to us like that," said the hipster husband.

Mia wrenched her arm out of Max's grip. "Two

weeks, Max. You don't call, you don't text, you don't tell me where you are or what you're doing. And now it suits you so I'm supposed to drop everything and come running? I don't think so!"

"We don't have time for this!" Max looked around, a sheen of sweat visible on his forehead. "Honey, we got to get going now. I'll explain everything, I promise." Max held out his hands. "I'm going to take you to Tahiti, buy you a mansion. Hell, I'll *build* you a mansion. We can stay up all night going over all my faults—but please, Mia, we gotta move it."

"Oh. My. God." Mia's eyes rounded. "It was you! Last night, the blackout—that was you!"

"Mia, you're talking crazy." Max looked over his shoulder. "She's talking crazy," he told the couple.

"I'm calling the police," said the woman.

"He's going to bolt." Clint stepped out from behind the sign. Out of the corners of his eyes, he saw Iron Man and Captain America move with him.

"Oh, sweet." The hipster man and woman both held up their iPhones to record the scene.

"Crap!" Max thrust out his hands, and there was a crackle of blue-white electricity. At almost the same instant, Iron Man pressed a button on his gauntlet, and the electricity arced backward, forming a translucent sphere around Max. "What the…" Falling back on his knees, Max reached out a tentative hand to touch the surface of the sphere. Energy crackled visibly; his finger hovered, not quite touching.

"I wouldn't if I were you," said Iron Man.

Max, clearly one of those kids who did precisely

what he was told not to, made contact. There was a sharp *bzzzzt* sound, and Max grunted and jerked back.

"Not too bright, are you?" Tony shook his head. "Now, talk to us."

Captain America knelt down, bringing his face close to Max's. "Who hired you? Who did you bring out?"

"Oh, man, no, this isn't happening, this can't be happening."

Mia pushed herself forward. "Why didn't you call me, Max?"

"Miss, you need to move back." Captain America pushed her gently but firmly to the side.

"Don't you manhandle me," said Mia. "I'll call my lawyer."

Max's head came up. "I want my lawyer! I'm not talking without my lawyer."

"You sure about that?" Clint moved closer to Max, still holding his arrow nocked and ready. "This is a specially designed arrowhead that will instantly short-circuit any electronic device. I figure if I hit you in the thigh, you'll short out and we can continue our little conversation."

"Hit me in the…" Max scuttled back, the sphere moving with him.

Clint tracked him with the arrow. "You don't have to keep still. I'm good with moving targets."

Max stumbled back against the side of the sphere, and his body arched again as energy coursed through him. His eyes rolled back in his head, and he slumped to the ground.

"Aw, that's just perfect." Iron Man released the button holding the sphere in place. Max remained immobile on the ground. "What are we going to do now?"

Captain America checked his pulse. "Still breathing. But I don't think we're going to get anything out of him tonight."

Clint took out his cellphone. "Yes, this is Special Agent Barton. We have Max Dillon contained. Can you send someone over to the Liberty Café at the… oh, you got it already? Great." He closed his phone.

"Max, are you okay?" Kneeling beside her unconscious boyfriend, Mia looked up at the hipster mom and dad, who were still holding out their iPhones. "Did you get all that? They threatened to shoot him with an arrow! That's brutality, right?"

"I would say so," said hipster dad. "Hey! Iron Man! Mind posing for a moment with my baby?"

As they left, Clint grabbed a fistful of freedom fries from a passing waiter's tray, just so the evening wouldn't prove a total loss.

NINE

THE prisoners were all drugged, of course, or else placed in Stark-designed restraints that neutralized their special abilities. Some of the most powerful, like Purple Man, were both drugged and collared, to keep them from breaking free of their standard-issue detainment cells. Two different human-rights organizations were already launching investigations into the treatment of the displaced prisoners. In the meantime, the forty-four recaptured Raft inmates were being held securely on Ryker's Island while their cells were repaired and, in some cases, rebuilt.

Peter knew all this, yet when he entered the corridor and looked down the rows of prisoners, he felt a blast of adrenaline that left him light-headed. Since he wasn't invulnerable, Peter was used to coming back home with a few cuts and bruises, but last night had been different. There was a moment, before Captain America and the others had reached him, when

Peter had been pretty sure he was going to die down here. And there was another moment when he had been pretty sure he wasn't going to die quickly enough.

"Hello, boys," he said. "Remember me?"

For a second, he felt as though he were back in high school, short and skinny and fair game for every bully who wanted to climb his way up the adolescent food chain. Peter had learned a valuable lesson back then, before acquiring his powers. The first time they hit you is a test. There's no real way to pass it—bullies don't usually walk away if you show no fear, they just hit you harder—but there's sure as hell a way to fail it.

"Well, well, look who came back for more," said Carnage. "Last night's dinner." His glassy blue eyes were human—as was his rawboned, freckled face. A heavy, high-tech collar flashed a sequence of lights in quick succession. Peter wondered what the mechanism did to inhibit the symbiote's power and figured Tony Stark knew the answer.

"What's the matter, Spider-Man? Did you get a taste for something rough?"

"Tell me the truth. You've been waiting your whole life to say that line, and now it feels a little hollow, right?"

It took Carnage a moment to think of a comeback. "Come a little closer and ask me that."

"Yeah, I thought so." Peter ambled along the path between the two rows of cells. "In fact, I'm betting you've all got a bad case of the morning-afters. You had a little taste of freedom last night…"

"Not to mention the joy of tenderizing you like a bad cut of meat," said Dr. Octopus, from the cell next to Carnage. Portly and bespectacled, the doctor seemed no more menacing than a gelded bull—but that was only because his articulated mechanical tentacles had been surgically removed from his abdomen.

Peter nodded. "And now, it's back to solitary amusements and a slab of nutraloaf on a napkin." Peter reached the end of the hallway, making sure all the inmates had gotten a good look at the brown cardboard box in his hands. "Kind of a shame you wasted so much time beating up on me, when you could have been making a run for it."

Carnage made a low, growling sound. "Big talker. What's in the box, Spider-Boy? Your..." He made a crude gesture with his hand.

"Actually, it's doughnuts."

"Doughnuts?"

"Last night, I bought myself this huge box of doughnuts from my favorite little coffee shop." Peter opened the box and let the sugary smell fill the air. "Now I'm thinking that I shouldn't go spoiling my girlish figure, so I'm wondering...does anyone else care for a doughnut?"

"Oh! Yes! Doughnut me!"

"Powdered sugar!"

"You got jelly?"

"Any of them chocolate?"

"Are those from Mike's coffee shop in Bay Ridge?" Dr. Octopus's myopic eyes grew teary behind his thick glasses. "I love their cinnamon rolls."

"Before I go handing out the treats, though, I have one little question." Peter paused, letting the grumbles and curses die down before continuing. "Who was behind last night?"

Silence.

"We already know that Electro did the wet work," said Peter. "What I want to know is, who came up with the plan?"

"Your mama," said Carnage.

"Ah, well," said Peter, "guess I'll just go leave these in the guards' lounge." He took one step toward the intercom, and then paused. "You were right, by the way, Otto. These are from Mike's."

He was facing the outer door when he heard someone say, "Lykos."

"Lykos."

"Karl Lykos."

"Shut up, Pigface, you're just repeating what I said."

"It was Karl Lykos, the doctor, now give me the damn doughnuts!"

Dr. Octopus pressed his pudgy face up against the bars. "If I tell you who went with him, can I get one of those big coffee roll things with the cinnamon?"

"Sorry, pal, I don't need any more help," said Peter. He handed out the doughnuts and left the prison, his mind racing.

Karl Lykos was a mutant with the ability to feed off other mutants' energy and shape-shift into a pteranodon. Since there weren't a lot of neighborhoods where prehistoric flying reptiles went unnoticed, Lykos made his home in the Savage Land, a tropical anomaly hidden deep in the remote continent of Antarctica. *Well,* Peter thought, *at least I don't have to waste time figuring out where to look for Lykos.* All he had to do was find a way to get to an inhospitable jungle on the other side of the world. Perched on top of the Roosevelt Island cable car, Peter thought longingly of home, tomato soup, saltines and ibuprofen, not necessarily in that order. He also thought about the likelihood that calling into work sick again was going to wind up with him getting fired from his teaching position at Midtown High. Of course, now that he wasn't getting married anymore, Peter didn't know whether he even wanted to keep the job. Truth was, he didn't know what he wanted.

But one thing was clear. He couldn't face Lykos on his own, not in his current weakened condition. Especially since Peter knew the doctor would be surrounding himself with friends and allies— if only to have a steady supply of food.

And if Peter didn't want a replay of his visit to the Raft, he was going to have to find some friends and allies of his own.

TEN

LUKE Cage was not the best person to sit next to on a small plane. First, there was the man's size. Second, there was his habit of sitting with his legs spread so wide that Peter had to keep his own legs at an angle to avoid touching the other man. Last, but not least, Luke was seriously on edge.

"I'm not saying I'm scared of flying," he said, not for the first time since they had taken off. "I'm saying, small planes are how God gets rid of excess rich people."

"I don't think Tony's your typical hobby pilot," said Peter. "Besides, he's got Captain America in the cockpit in case anything goes wrong."

Luke's eyes rounded. "Wrong? What do you think's going to go wrong?"

"Nothing. Besides, what are you worrying about? You're pretty near invulnerable. It's Jessica and Clint and yours truly who are liable to become Hamburger Helper if we crash."

"Hey," said Clint, from the other side of the aisle. "What's wrong with Hamburger Helper? I make a mean tortilla casserole with that stuff."

Luke gave Peter a hard look. "Do. Not. Talk. About. Crashing."

"Sorry." Peter settled back into his chair and took out a copy of *New York* magazine. As he scanned the Brilliant/Despicable list, he could feel Luke still staring at him, but tried to ignore it.

"Are you really going to sit there in that mask for the whole flight?"

Without missing a beat, Peter said, "Are you really going to wear that little wooly yellow cap?"

"My wooly cap says I want to keep my bald head warm. Your mask says you don't trust me. So how do you expect us to work together?"

"I'm not expecting anything from anyone. I rely on myself." Peter tried to keep a note of smugness from creeping into his voice, but it was difficult. After all that trouble, Electro had turned out not to know that Lykos had hired him. Tony Stark might be a billionaire genius, but it was Peter's hunch that had produced the goods.

"Then you're not part of this team," said Luke. "You go into a battle situation with people, you are supposed to expect something from them, and they are supposed to expect something from you. You want to keep to yourself? Fine. But you're putting the whole mission in jeopardy."

Behind his mask, Peter felt himself flush with anger. "I'm sorry, *Power Man*, but it's not just *my* safety I'm worried about."

"You think no one else has anyone they want to protect? Please. You go ahead and hide whatever you're hiding under there, but do not try to tell me it's about other people. I got a pregnant wife back home. So either take off the mask and tell me your first name, or don't expect me to have your back."

Peter stood up, ready to change seats, and bumped into Jessica, who was putting something in the overhead compartment. "Sorry," he said, sitting back down. She was dressed in a skintight red-and-yellow Spider-Woman suit that was actually quite modest—or would have been, on a woman with a less Amazonian figure. "Where are you sitting?" he asked.

"Next to Clint. Why?"

Peter didn't look at Luke. "No reason."

Luke gave a little bark of laughter. "You want to switch seats, Spider-Man? Did I hurt your feelings? I must be crazy, heading off to some land-that-time-forgot jungle in the middle of Antarctica. I mean, what kind of idiot would choose to hide out in a place where they have dinosaurs running around, anyhow?"

"A guy who turns into a dinosaur," said Peter.

"Lykos isn't the only escaped Raft inmate who was based in the Savage Land prior to capture," said Jessica, tapping on her computer. "I'm betting Mandrill and Nekra will be heading back there, as well."

Luke shook his head. "I was in high school when the first reports came out. I remember telling my friend that he was full of it. Some British guy discovers a real-life Jurassic Park inside a ring of live volcanoes? I told him, 'Give Elvis and Bigfoot my regards.'"

"Weird was my normal," said Jessica. "I've got more of a problem believing that there are normal people living the kind of lives you see on sitcoms."

"Always imagined going there someday, though." Luke smiled sheepishly. "Thought I'd get to ride a Brontosaurus or something, like Fred Flintstone."

"Apatosaurus," said Peter. "Yeah, I remember my tenth-grade science teacher telling us when the U.N. declared the region out of bounds for any commercial or tourist purposes. I think I sulked for a week."

"Jeez, you were in tenth grade?" Luke laughed. "I was already serving time."

"Hey boys and girl." Steve, who had been sitting next to Tony in the cockpit, moved down the center aisle like a coach addressing his team before a big game. Steve was wearing his Captain America shirt with a pair of pressed khakis, and he looked so blond and square-jawed and clean-cut, he made Peter feel that perhaps pressed khakis were the answer to everything. "How is everyone doing back here?"

"Just peachy," said Luke, his voice gravely. "My wife is liable to give birth any day, and I'm running off to save the world with a bunch of people I hardly know."

"You know me," said Jessica. "And your wife's not due for another month."

"*If* everything goes according to plan," said Luke. "In my life? Things do not tend to go according to plan."

"I've got a plan," said Tony, swiveling in the pilot's seat to face them. With his stubbled goatee, Black Sabbath T-shirt and the silver bracelet on his left wrist, Tony looked more like a dissolute rock star from the eighties than a billionaire genius. "We land, we find the bad guys, we kick their asses. On the way back, we stop off at the Quay in Sydney to try their tasting menu. Last time, I had hand-caught Tasmanian squid and wild grey ghost mushrooms."

Steve nodded. "That's a swell idea, Tony, but where exactly are we going to start looking? We're talking about a jungle. It's not like Lykos is going to be making cash withdrawals or get caught on someone's security camera."

Tony turned back to the instrument panel, flicked a button, then turned back. "You know how the X-Men have a gizmo for detecting mutant energy signatures?"

"Cerebro," said Steve. "I've heard of it. It takes a telepath to operate, right?"

"And it's stuck in a dedicated chamber. I've just improved it by making it mobile and changing the specs so you don't have to be a mind-reader to use it. You do have to have an IQ of over 175, however. I call it Analytica."

"That's a terrible name," said Peter. "Sounds like an accounting app."

"I know. If you have any better suggestions, I'm open to input." Tony swiveled back to face the cockpit. "Hang on, that's strange."

"Oh, dear God," said Luke, gripping the sides of his seat. "What's wrong?"

"I've been trying to take a look at Lykos's file, and there's something a little hinky about it." Tony tapped something on a laptop opened on the co-pilot's seat to the left of him. "Huh. It has a security lock on it."

Luke grabbed Peter's arm. "This is what I was talking about. He's checking Lykos's file while he's flying. You know what happens to people who multitask like that?"

Peter looked out the window. There were a lot of puffy white clouds. "I don't think we're going to crash into anything at the moment, Luke."

Luke nodded three times, as if Peter had just confirmed his worst suspicions. "I must be going crazy."

"Let me have a look at that file," said Jessica. Opening up her laptop, she typed in a few codes. "Nothing. If it were coded in AES—Advanced Encryption Standard cipher algorithm—that would open it. But it's not."

"So it's protected by something stronger than the code that safeguards most diplomatic exchanges and financial transactions," said Tony. "That's interesting, in a 'Gee, wonder why the husband of the missing woman cleaned his car trunk with bleach' kind of way."

Jessica tapped her fingernail against the computer. "I don't have the clearance to override this, Cap. Do you?"

"I should be able to." Steve leaned over and punched in a code. "That's odd."

"Let me try something else," said Jessica, typing. Suddenly she paused and sat back, looking stunned. "Huh."

Clint, seated beside her, leaned in. "What do you see?"

"The S.H.I.E.L.D. outpost in the Savage Land is offline."

"I take it that's not exactly normal?"

"They're never supposed to go offline. The purpose of the facility is to intercept, store and analyze intelligence data." Jessica stared at the computer as though it had just turned into something strange and potentially dangerous. Peter felt a prickle of alarm.

"Maybe you should try to contact them," said Luke.

"Better not," said Peter. "Someone locks Lykos's file, and Lykos organizes a prison break. We're following him back to his home in the Savage Land, and now we've got a S.H.I.E.L.D. outpost here that's gone dark. Call me a paranoid conspiracy-theory guy, but it seems to me that these things could be connected."

Luke frowned. "What if they're all sick or something? They could have gotten some crazy Savage virus."

"That's possible," said Steve. "Or they could have some kind of security breach inside the compound. If they were under attack, the first thing they would do is shut down."

Peter could see that everyone was thinking the same thing: The situation had just gotten a lot more complicated.

"Anyone consider that this could be some super-secret S.H.I.E.L.D. op?" Luke tore open a packet of nuts and popped one into his mouth. "They may hire me from time to time, but I can't say I trust any organization that has its fingers in as many pies as S.H.I.E.L.D. does."

"I don't trust organizations, period," said Peter, holding out his hand.

"Finally, we agree on something. For that, you get three nuts." He shook them into Peter's hand.

"You guys are wrong," said Steve. "I'm not saying that S.H.I.E.L.D. is perfect, and there are always some bad eggs, but they're working to promote democratic ideals."

"You want to know my philosophy?" Tony turned in the pilot's chair, looking over his shoulder at the others. "Give S.H.I.E.L.D. the benefit of the doubt, and keep the very latest technology advances to myself."

"If you feel that way," said Jessica, "why did you even bother to include us? We work for S.H.I.E.L.D., remember?"

"We've all worked for S.H.I.E.L.D., except Spider-Man," said Clint. "The question is, have we drunk the Kool-Aid? Speaking for myself, the answer is no. Now, where did you get those nuts from?"

"Check the pocket with the crash-safety instructions." Luke crumpled the empty packaging in his hand. "Well, at least now we know where to look for the were-dino-vamp," said Luke. "He's probably having a luau at the S.H.I.E.L.D. outpost."

Peter shook his head. "Not unless they're mutants. As far as I know, Lykos is on a strict mutant-only diet." There was silence as everyone thought about the implications of this: Lykos had no reason to keep non-mutants alive.

"Okay," said Clint, "so we have two objectives here: get a sit-rep on the S.H.I.E.L.D. outpost and track down Lykos and friends."

Jessica clicked her computer mouse and brought up a topographical map of the Savage Land, prompting a heated debate about mission priorities, assignments and strategies. After a few minutes of this, Peter excused himself to go the bathroom.

Locking the door behind him, he pulled off his mask and splashed cold water on his face. His left eye was still puffy and mostly shut, but the skin around it had faded from black to purple.

All of a sudden, Peter remembered a pre-spider-bite summer-adventure trip he had taken to Costa Rica as a teen. All the other kids had been running up and down the airplane aisles, laughing with friends, singing, telling loud stories. Sitting in his seat with his nose pressed to the window, Peter had wondered what was wrong with him. A few months later, he had acquired his powers. In a way that hadn't made him different as much as it had given him an easy excuse for not fitting in.

Yet here he was, with a bunch of people who were supposed to be his peers, and Peter didn't feel like he fit in here, either. *Shake it off, Parker.* Peter looked at the mask in his hands, and then deliberately kept it off as he left the bathroom.

As he made his way back to his seat, he heard Steve saying, "All right, folks. I suggest you try and close your eyes while you can. After we get there, we're not going to have much chance for sleep. Also, once we begin to make our descent, you'll have to assume crash positions. There's some kind of atmospheric barrier around the Savage Land that plays havoc with flight systems, so we should anticipate a rough landing."

Luke moved so Peter could slide into the window seat, his eyes skimming Peter's bare, bruised face. "You look like hell."

"We can't all have unbreakable skin." He fastened his seat belt. "You can call me Peter. Or Pete. Just not Petey."

Luke pulled off his yellow wool cap and handed it to Peter. "Here you go."

"I don't want your hat, Luke."

"That's 'cause you got no personal style. Go on. Take it."

After looking at it for a moment, Peter threw it backward, to Jessica.

"Hey," said Clint, "did anyone lose a yellow hat?"

"It's mine," said Luke, holding up a hand. "May I have it back, please?"

"Sure," said Clint, balling it up and throwing it into the cockpit. "Woops, missed."

"Guys," said Steve. He held up the yellow hat, looking like a camp counselor who had just discovered his charges had vandalized the bathrooms with toothpaste and toilet paper. "I don't know what you think you're doing, but these are very complicated controls here."

"Actually, they're quite simple," said Tony. "Part of my genius design."

"Oh," said Steve. "Well, in that case…"

Luke didn't get his hat back for a long time. When he did, it was three sizes too big for his head. He didn't complain, though, and Peter decided he didn't entirely dislike his seatmate.

THE first sign of trouble was a pocket of turbulence that made the plane lurch up and down. Luke, who had fallen asleep with headphones in his ears and a copy of *What to Expect When You're Expecting* on his lap, snapped awake, knocking his elbow into Peter's bruised rib.

"Sorry," he said, as the plane began to shake violently.

"No problem, I'll just put my head between my knees and retch my guts out," said Peter. Suddenly, Tony and Steve started arguing.

"Don't get your panties in a twist," said Tony. "We're going to land this baby so gently you can all put in your contact lenses."

"Watch it, Tony!"

"The wheel's not responding the way it…"

"Use the instruments, not the visuals. That mountain's much closer than it looks."

"Don't tell me how to fly this plane. I invented this plane."

"I don't think that position looks right…something's messing with the altimeter."

Luke and Peter stared at each other. From the other side of the aisle, they could hear Jessica saying, "Clint, there's something I really think you should know…" when the plane bounced abruptly. A siren went off, and all the overhead compartments snapped open.

Next to Peter, Luke was cursing so softly it sounded like a prayer.

There was a bump as the landing gear touched

down, followed by a high whine as the brakes engaged. Then, to Peter's surprise, the plane slowed and came to a surprisingly gentle stop.

For a moment, everything was quiet. "Well," said Tony, standing up and looking a little pale and sweaty in his black T-shirt and jeans. "Welcome to the Savage Land. On behalf of myself and my flight attendant here, we thank you for flying with us today." He pressed a button on a silver bracelet around his left wrist and a compartment door slid open in the floor of the cockpit, revealing the Iron Man armor. As if magnetized, the leg pieces rotated and flew onto Tony's legs, snapping into place. The other pieces followed, fitting themselves together with astonishing speed.

"Okay, everyone," said Steve, "time to gather up your equipment."

Luke stood up. "I don't know about you, but I am going to take a minute to use the bathroom."

"My foot fell asleep."

Peter felt a tingling sense of unease, and then a full-scale premonition of impending disaster. "Guys," he said. "We have to get off this plane now."

"What are you talking about, Pete?"

"I've got a bad feeling."

"Okay, everyone, let's move it," said Steve. "If Peter says he senses something, I trust him."

"Me, too," said Jessica.

Outside the plane, Peter was hit by the heavy, fetid, overly sweet scent of overripe and rotting vegetation.

Tony had managed to land the plane in a small clearing, but there was a dense tree canopy all around them, roped and knotted with thick vines and fleshy, shiny leaves. The air was so humid it was difficult to breathe, let alone speak, and Peter wondered whether this was contributing to his rising sense of alarm.

Jessica came up to Peter and put her hand on his arm. "What is it, Pete?"

"I'm not sure."

"Should we…"

"Wait." And then they heard something crashing through the trees toward them, its shrill screams filling the air. The moment before it came into view, Peter braced himself, knowing the first danger in facing a monster was freezing out of sheer surprise. *All right, you big ugly reptile*, he thought, *come out and play.*

Only it wasn't a giant reptile that came bursting out of the tree cover, cocking its head and looking down at them from its malevolent little eyes.

It was a bird.

ELEVEN

"SWEET Christmas," said Luke. "What is that thing? Big Bird on steroids?"

"They're called terror birds," said Jessica.

"Phorusrhacid," corrected Tony, his voice sounding robotic through the Iron Man helmet. "Part of a clade of large, carnivorous, flightless birds distantly related to modern-day falcons and parrots."

"Hey, Polly," said Luke. "Want a cracker?" He cracked the knuckles of his right hand. The seven-foot-tall terror bird turned to Luke, ruffling the dark gray feathers at its neck and cocking its head.

Clint had an arrow nocked and was tracking the bird. "What's it doing?"

"Weighing its various dinner options," said Peter. The bird fixed its beady eyes on him, opened its huge, sharply curved beak and gave a shrill cry. "It seems the customer would like one Spider-Man fillet, extremely rare."

Clint let the arrow fly as the terror bird raced toward Peter; the arrow caught the bird in the side, but didn't even make the powerful legs falter in their stride. Clint raced alongside, nocking another arrow as he ran. The bird's claws looked as sharp as its beak, and Clint hoped he wouldn't have to get too close to either end of the creature.

"Tony," Clint called out, "think you can—" He broke off as more terror birds, a whole flock of them, attacked at once. Captain America flung his shield at a bird that was launching itself at Jessica, but Jessica was rolling to the side while shooting, and the shield intercepted one of her bullets. Iron Man was airborne, lifting another of the giant birds by the tail. Unfortunately, the creature still had Luke's arm gripped firmly in its beak.

"Tony," Luke shouted, dangling twenty feet off the ground, "you're not helping me, here!"

Tony punched the bird in the beak and it released Luke, who fell to the ground rolling and came up on the balls of his feet. "You okay?"

Luke spat out a mouthful of dust. "Just don't do me any more favors."

Obviously, they still hadn't quite gotten the knack of working as a team.

Clint fired three arrows at the bird chasing Peter— hitting it in the left wing, neck and rump—and swore under his breath as the bird reacted by increasing its speed. Clint wanted to select one of his special arrows, but he couldn't manipulate the quiver while sprinting. Then Peter angled toward a stand of trees, stopped running and began firing off webbing at the lowest hanging branches. For a moment, Clint thought he'd lost his mind. Then he realized what Peter was doing: He was stringing his web into a net. The only problem was, he was never going to get it finished in time. Peter glanced over his shoulder and began to work more quickly, weaving the strands more loosely.

"Clint? Do me a favor," said Peter, holding his ground as the terror birds galloped closer and closer. "Don't tell anyone I ran from a giant chicken?"

"Sorry, man. I already posted the picture on Facebook."

At the last minute, Peter sprang up into the closest tree, leaving the birds to race straight into the net. "Hey," Clint said, "I think you did it."

"Yeah," said Peter. "I think I—oh, crap." One bird tore a hole in the net with its sharp beak and lunged at Peter. Clint shot one more arrow; this time, he got a clean shot through the bird's brain. It shrieked and fell to the ground.

Clint looked around. Tony was blasting down to earth while Steve wiped clotted feathers off his shield. "I think that was the last one."

"You know," said Peter as they caught their breath, "I kind of imagined being part of a super-powered team meant *less* running for your life. And it's not as though we got attacked by a T-rex, either."

"I guess that's what you get when you put together a team of loners." As he spoke, Clint scanned the field. He spotted Luke crouching down beside a badly in-jured terror bird, snapping its neck to put it out of its misery. There was no sign of Jessica, however, and Clint began doing a more systematic search, mentally breaking the field into a grid.

Nothing. She was gone.

"We got to get out of here," said Luke as Clint approached. "All that screaming is like putting out a big fat 'dinner is served' sign for every predator in earshot."

"Jessica's missing," said Clint, his eyes moving over the field again, searching for any sign of red. Thank God she was wearing her bright Spider-Woman costume instead of the dark S.H.I.E.L.D. jumpsuit. "Do you think another bird got her?"

"I didn't see any more birds," said Luke. "And they're kind of hard to miss."

"I'll do a flyover of the entire area," said Tony, beginning to rise up off the ground.

Just then, there was a distinctively feminine shriek of pain from the dense tropical undergrowth behind them. Clint pulled a small survival knife out of its sheath and hacked at the thick vegetation, his jaw set as he prepared himself for the worst.

What he saw was so unexpected, he burst out laughing. Instead of being attacked by a terror bird, Jessica was straddling the Black Widow.

Jess's black hair and red-and-yellow costume formed a perfect contrast with the smaller woman's black body armor and auburn hair. Jessica bore down on Natasha's arm, pressing Natasha's own sharply bladed throwing star against her throat. Unfazed by this, Natasha was biting off a bunch of angry-sounding Russian, and Clint didn't need a

Ph.D. in Slavic languages to guess what the last word meant.

"Well, how was I to know you were trying not to hurt me?" Jessica did not release the other woman's arm. "You snuck up behind me and held a blade against my throat!"

"I didn't recognize you with the mask and costume," said Natasha, a hint of accent coming through. "I thought you might be one of Lykos's mutate gang."

"Jessica, I think you can let her up now," said Steve.

Tony gave the other man a sour look. "Spoilsport."

Jessica didn't budge. "Not until someone else secures her. She tried to slit my throat."

"She's not going anywhere," said Steve, his hand on Jessica's shoulder. "Let her go." He tugged, and Jessica reluctantly rolled off the Widow. "So you took her down? Nice work."

Clint looked at his partner, but it was hard to tell what she was thinking behind the red mask covering her eyes. "Thanks, but to be honest, I think her fighting skills have been exaggerated."

Natasha's green eyes narrowed. "And yours have been understated. I was told you didn't have any powers."

"I don't," said Jessica, brushing at the grass stains on her knees. "So stop looking for excuses."

Natasha raised her eyebrows, patently disbelieving. "Oh, really? You're saying you overpowered me without using any special abilities?"

Jessica shrugged. "Sorry, honey. Sometimes the truth hurts."

Clint, who was watching Natasha, grabbed her a moment before she would have attacked. The redhead struggled against his grip. "*Durak!* Can't you tell she's lying? You fought me yourself, remember. Is she really better at hand-to-hand combat than you are?"

Clint didn't say anything, but registered the fact that Jessica had managed to subdue Natasha much more quickly than he had, back on the Helicarrier. Maybe Jess was just a better fighter than he had realized; maybe she'd had the advantage of surprise. Still, he wouldn't have thought Jessica could defeat him without her powers—and not, he hoped, just because he was a macho jerk.

"Let her go," said Jessica. "She wants another round? Fine by me."

"Forget it," said Steve, his voice pitched halfway between camaraderie and command. "We've got a lot of work to do here, and this is not exactly a day in the park." He gestured around them at the clusters of tall umbrella pines and hickory and oak trees, which could have hidden a herd of angry mammoths in their dark shadows. "We're liable to get eaten by something while you two go at each other."

"If you let her go, she's going to run back to Lykos and tell him where we are," said Jessica.

"I'm not *with* Lykos. I came here tracking Lykos." Natasha looked over her shoulder at Clint. "You can let go of me now."

Clint released Natasha's arms. "So we're supposed to

believe you happened to notice Lykos leaving the Raft and just decided to go after him?"

Natasha moved so her back was to a tree and she could see all the other members of the group. "Most of the inmates were just breaking and running. Lykos moved deliberately, like he had a plan. I saw him down by the dock, meeting up with the Albino witch-woman and the baboon man and a few of the others, and it seemed to me that they didn't all just happen to bump into each other there."

There were murmurs as the others took this in.

"So why did you even care?" Jessica moved so Natasha had to turn her head to see her. "I would have thought you only cared for paying gigs."

"I'm not pretending to be altruistic," said Natasha. "But I'm a long-view investor. And as you know, I'm considering the advantages of working with your side."

"Uh-huh," said Clint. "And how exactly did you make it to the Savage Land without Lykos's assistance? It's not as if you could just hop on a commercial flight." Clint leaned against another tree and folded his arms across his chest, more interested in reading the Widow's expression than in hearing her response.

"How did I get on the Helicarrier? I have my ways," said Natasha, folding her throwing star up and replacing it in her utility belt. "Maybe I could teach you a few tricks."

"I say we work together," said Tony, raising his face-plate and walking over to Natasha's side. "In fact, I'd be willing to work very, very closely with—what did you say your name was?"

"Natasha Romanova," said Clint, "and she's working with me." Jessica gave him a look that said she thought he'd lost his mind, but Clint didn't care. Let them all think the Black Widow had ensnared him. He had his own reasons for sticking close to the Russian spy.

If she was working for Lykos, it was his responsibility to make sure she didn't deliver them into the doctor's hands. He had disobeyed Hill's orders to kill the Widow rather than permit her to escape; if it looked like he'd made a mistake in letting Natasha live, Clint knew he had to correct that mistake. And soon.

CLINT kept one eye on Natasha as he passed around chunks of roasted terror bird. He figured the leaping flames would keep the local wildlife from attacking, but there was no question the aroma of roasting fowl was attracting a bit of attention. As the shadows lengthened, there were shrill cries and hoots from the tree canopy, and the rustling of some arborial creature moving through the leafy branches overhead. Because it was late November in the Southern hemisphere, the sun was just beginning to set even though it was only an hour before midnight. There would only be a few hours of darkness before it rose again, which meant none of them would be getting much sleep.

Which was probably for the best, considering they

were in a jungle surrounded by dinosaurs, mutated beast people, and various hostile tribes. On the other hand, lack of sleep wouldn't help the team's mood, which was already a bit low. After the terror birds had been dispatched, they had wasted half a day tracking down false readings from Tony's mutant-energy detector, and now they were all exhausted and cranky.

Well, at least they weren't going hungry. "Anyone want more terror bird?"

"Not after watching you rip its head off," said Peter. "I'm fine with the freeze-dried beef stew, thanks."

"I guess I'll have another piece," said Luke, walking up to the spit where the enormous fowl crackled with savory juices. A few feathers still clung to the wings and legs; every once in a while, someone would spit out a feather that had floated back on the tropical breeze.

"So, Tony, you got any idea why that gizmo of yours didn't work?" Luke gestured with his giant drumstick. "'Cause I do not want to spend any more time running around in circles."

"There's only one possible explanation." Tony looked up, a tiny screwdriver in his hands and one of his gauntlets on his lap. A panel was open, revealing some of the complicated circuitry inside. "Lykos must be inside some sort of structure containing large amounts of Vibranium. That's the only thing that could throw the sensors off."

"Okay, so that should narrow it down," said Luke, taking another bite. "How many Vibranium buildings does this place have?"

"A few, actually," said Steve. "The Savage Land is one of the biggest sources of naturally occurring Vibranium, so it's been used to build some of the science stations."

"I saw something on the map," said Jessica, standing up and stretching. "The ruins of a citadel."

"It's worth checking out. And then there's the S.H.I.E.L.D. outpost." Clint was very aware of Natasha, sitting quietly by his side and taking all this in.

A snapped twig made everyone jump. Luke threw down his drumstick and got to his feet. "Okay, what was that?"

"That was me," said Peter, holding up his hands. "You going to shoot anyone who goes to the bathroom?"

"Sorry, I'm used to urban jungles." Luke picked his drumstick off the ground, and then threw it into the fire. "Put me in a neighborhood so bad even the rats are scared to come out at night, I'm fine. But I didn't spend my summers hiking and camping."

"It's not exactly my comfort zone, either," said Peter, groaning a little as he sat back down on the ground. "Swinging through trees instead of buildings uses a different set of muscles."

"What a bunch of whiners," said Tony. "Maybe we should call our team the Urban Avengers, and explain that we just can't take on any jobs outside a major metropolitan area." He had peeled off his armor and was wearing a white undershirt that showed the shape of the mini-reactor embedded in the center of his chest. "I'm so sorry the bad guys decamped into a swamp," he continued in a breathy falsetto, "but dealing with wildlife just isn't in my contract."

"You think I'm scared of wildlife?" Luke's voice was so low it sounded like a growl. "Last month I had to deal with six Cane Corsos, bio-engineered with Adamantium bones and teeth and no inhibitions against attacking humans." Luke pulled a toothpick out of his pocket and stuck it in his mouth. "Peter might be a pampered city slicker, but I deal with wildlife all the time." He glanced sideways at Peter, the only clue that he was playing with him.

"Yeah, anyone can be tough when they don't get so much as a scratch." Peter unzipped the neck of his costume and pulled it down enough to reveal the livid bruises on his ribs. "And my wrist is broken."

Jessica winced a little. "Oh, Peter, ouch."

"Spare me your sob stories." Tony pulled up his jeans leg. "Take a look at that."

Luke, collecting plates, cast an amused glance over his shoulder. "At what? Your skinny white chicken legs?"

"No, my skinny *pink* chicken leg, where a crazy volcano lady tried to melt off my flesh. It goes all the way up to my thighs. Let me tell you, a little cut or bump does not compare to a third-degree burn close to the family jewels."

Jessica handed Luke her plate. "Guess you weren't wearing your armor, huh?"

Tony shrugged. "What can I say? She was a very attractive crazy volcano lady."

"Well, if we're playing 'I'll show you mine if you show me yours…'" Jessica pulled back her long black hair. "See this?" She pointed to a thin, almost un-noticeable scar near her hairline. "That's where Dr. Octopus tried to scalp me."

"No kidding," said Steve, pulling back his hair. "I've got one of those, too, from Arnim Zola. He was trying to extract my brain so he could use my body for his own devices."

"Who could blame him," murmured Jessica, and Steve looked so startled that Clint nearly fell over laughing. "What scars have you got, Hawkeye?"

Clint, very aware of the quiet Russian woman sitting by his side, considered which scars he felt like exposing. It was all well and good for folks to show off their little dings and marks, but Clint had suffered some injuries that had required surgery and physical therapy, and he didn't want to reveal any potential weaknesses. "Well, for starters, I've got this." He opened his leather vest, revealing the jagged, raised tangle of scar tissue over his heart.

"Jesus," said Peter, "what caused that?"

"Broken glass," said Natasha, her voice very quiet. With her bare hand, she traced the scar, and Clint gave an involuntary shiver before grabbing her wrist. "How did you get this?"

"Same as everyone else, I got it in a fight."

Natasha's gaze seemed far too knowing for Clint's comfort. "And what was the name of your adversary?"

Clint hesitated, and then thought, what the hell? "I didn't know his name. It wasn't that kind of a fight."

"Ah." Her nod said she understood what he wasn't saying: His scar hadn't come from some super-powered adversary in a colorful costume. It had come from a much less glamorous, much darker kind of battle. And it had come from a time before Clint had the skills to protect himself.

"How about you, Ms. Romanova," said Jessica. "Do you have any scars you'd like to show us?"

Natasha hesitated, and then unzipped the front of her black jumpsuit. Underneath, Clint saw, she wore a serviceable, modest black sports bra that couldn't completely flatten the generous curve of her breasts. "I have this," she said, pulling aside the strap to show the v-shaped scar just below her collarbone. She met his eyes, and he understood what she was revealing: a childhood not entirely unlike his own.

"Mine's bigger," he said.

Natasha pulled back the sleeves of her black jumpsuit. Clint took her arm in his hands and examined the tiny, almost invisible cuts on her palm and the soft inside of her forearm. She showed him the other arm; the marks were more visible there.

"Defensive cuts. How old were you?"

"They say I was seven," said Natasha, with a shrug. "But that's a guess. I was small for my age for a long time, so I might well have been older."

There was a popping sound from the fire, but no one else spoke. Without thinking, Clint stroked his thumb across the marks on the tender skin of Natasha's forearm. Then, realizing what he was doing, Clint dropped his hand, grabbed his bow and laid it across his lap so he could wipe it down.

"Didn't you already clean that?"

Clint didn't dare look at Jessica. "I don't tell you how to care for your gun, do I?"

Jessica stood up from Clint's side. "Tony," she said, sitting back down next to him, "have you had any luck hacking into Lykos's file?"

"Still locked, but I've got an automatic system going that keeps running through different combinations of passwords. The S.H.I.E.L.D. outpost is still offline, by the way."

Jessica's eyes cut to the Black Widow, and then away. "Yes, they'll probably remain that way for another two to four hours, as part of the training exercise."

Tony glanced up at Jessica, and then quickly over at Natasha. "Yeah, the training exercise. I forgot."

Clint tried not to laugh. For a genius, Tony could sure be slow on the uptake. Clint didn't think the Widow had been fooled by any of that for an instant. Jessica and Tony continued to discuss hacking strategies.

Clint knew by the set of Jessica's jaw that she was pissed off at him. The next time they all sat down together, Jessica would not be at his side. *I'm not some teenage jerk trying to get into the new girl's pants,* he wanted to say. *I'm a S.H.I.E.L.D. assassin trying to determine if I have to take her out.* But that didn't quite explain the hot rush that had swept through Clint at the touch of the Russian's arm. *Her arm, for crying out loud.* If it hadn't all been so deadly serious, it would have been hysterically funny.

All of a sudden, everyone seemed to fall silent, and Clint grew aware of the chorus of chirping frogs that filled the evening air, punctuated by something making a rhythmic percussive sound on a tree.

"All right," said Tony. "Here's what I think. At first light, I'll make a quick aerial pass over the science compounds, the S.H.I.E.L.D. outpost and the citadel."

"I have to disagree," said Steve. "If Lykos and whoever is with him spot you overhead, we lose the element of surprise. And there must be a million ways to lose yourself in the jungle. We need to be stealthy." He took a stick and scratched a crude map of the area. "There are three big science compounds—two of them located on remote islands, one on the top of a mountain. In addition, we need to do a recon of the citadel and the S.H.I.E.L.D. outpost. So that's five potential targets and six of us."

"Seven," said Natasha.

"You're not one of us," said Jessica. "Captain, I think either Clint or I should check out the S.H.I.E.L.D. outpost."

"Both of you go together. Luke, I think you and Peter should head toward the ruined citadel. I'll investigate the southern science compound."

Tony closed the panel on his gauntlet. "I take it you want me to handle the two island locations?"

"Since you can travel underwater, yes, I think that makes the most sense."

Tony pointed at the dirt map. "You do know we have laptops?"

"Force of habit." Steve used the stick to wipe away the markings. "Now, we should try to get some rest.

We're going to have a long day tomorrow."

Clint nodded. "Who's going to take first watch?"

"My armor has a built-in intruder alert," said Tony, setting his helmet on a rock. "Keep an eye open, armor."

The helmet's eyes lit up. "Affirmative, Mr. Stark."

"Wake us if we have any uninvited guests." Tony handed out thin sleeping bag rolls made of a Stark-designed technical material. One by one, the new Avengers spread out their sleeping bags on the ground, settled in around the campfire and closed their eyes, trying to take advantage of what remained of the night. For some, sleep came more easily than others. For Clint, it never came at all—which turned out to be a very good thing.

TWELVE

UNDER the cover of darkness, while Captain America kept watch for external threats, Natasha slipped out of the Avengers' camp. She moved with exquisite caution, transferring her weight with a dancer's lightness, timing her steps to coincide with the calls of distant animals or the rustling of wind through the trees. As she reached a safe distance from the others, she was surprised by the pang of regret she felt as she left the warmth and relative safety of the fire behind. *Of course*, she mocked herself, *it's the fire you'll miss, and not a certain sharp-eyed archer who saw far too much for your comfort.* What was even more unsettling, he seemed to understand what he saw. As Natasha had learned back in her applied-psychology practicum, the sense of being understood is extremely seductive. Beauty may attract, eroticism may ensnare, but it is the conviction that one is truly and intimately comprehended by another that creates a sense of trust.

And without trust, there can be no betrayal—a spy's real purpose.

His thumb brushing over her old scars. So clever, to act as though it had been an inadvertent touch, to drop his hand so abruptly, as if he hadn't known what he was doing. It had been so very effective that Natasha knew she must try it herself. And the look in his eyes—how had he managed that perfect balance between wariness and warmth? Most convincing. It had almost gotten to her. No. It *had* gotten to her—just a little, just for a moment—before she remembered her training.

Natasha tripped over a tree root, and then froze, listening intently. *Nothing.* She was alone. And that was as it should be. The Black Widow did not go around missing fires and companionship and petty thieves turned sharpshooters who were not even the strongest in the group, who were not even the cleverest or the most handsome. He wasn't even particularly tall, for crying out loud.

She could just imagine what Yelena would have said: "He looks like a construction worker who expects some little woman to serve him steaming plates of Pelmeni while he gets drunk on cheap street vodka." If only she could talk to Yelena, Natasha knew she could shake this absurd attraction. But Yelena was still in the program, and Natasha couldn't think of any safe way to contact her best friend.

Distracted, Natasha suddenly found herself caught in a tangle of vines; she had to take a few moments to extricate herself. The tropical night was still almost pitch black, and Natasha could barely make out the little glow-in-the-dark compass she had lifted from Hawkeye's gear while he slept. No matter. The main thing was to get back to Lykos's camp and establish some sort of cover before dawn.

Natasha tripped again, this time over something that hissed. She paused, her heart pounding, wondering whether she should wait till there was more light.

No, she thought, *best to keep pressing onward*. She wondered how many nocturnal predators there were in this place. She had never felt so unprepared for an assignment. She was usually thoroughly briefed by her bosses, but here she was on her own, with limited resources. From what she had pieced together, the Savage Land contained an odd assortment of dinosaurs from several different prehistoric periods, along with saber-tooths and other mammals from the Ice Age. The big birds that had attacked the others were actually from an earlier period—after the great extinction event that had ended the age of giant reptiles, but before the change in climate that had brought the giant mammals to the very top of the food chain.

All in all, the Savage Land might look like a wild jungle, but it was a thoroughly artificial construct, created by some alien who had gone about collecting life-forms with more enthusiasm than discipline— like a child capriciously choosing incompatible fish to fill his tank. What did the child care if one fish began to decimate all his companions? He was off to play with other toys.

There was a snuffling sound from the bushes, and Natasha fingered the gun she had managed to steal from Jessica's pack. It was only a little Glock 26, but it was better than relying entirely on the prison-made throwing star she had swiped from a Raft inmate. The snuffling animal emerged, revealing itself as a little porcine creature, rooting through the soil and leaves for insects and grubs.

Natasha berated herself for her nerves, but her heart was still beating faster than usual. She knew how many men she could take on and win, but she had no illusions about how she might fare in a head-to-head battle with a Tyrannosaurus rex.

Maybe you should just go back and try your luck with Hawkeye and the rest. It was such a tempting option, Natasha knew instantly she must resist it. They did not trust her, and Jessica knew Natasha was on to her—which made Jessica particularly dangerous. *I shouldn't have said what I did about her powers—that was stupid of me. A misstep.* It would be very easy for Jessica to use some battle as an excuse to attempt to rid herself of Natasha.

And then there was the question of Clint himself. He was the hardest of the group to read. Her instinct was that Clint was dangerous to her now in a way he had not been before. Back at the Raft, he had kept her in his line of vision, and he had done the same thing around the campfire. But now Natasha sensed a guardedness in him, and a resolve, that seemed different. He wanted *her*, that had not changed, but desire had never stopped her from ruthlessly executing a target. There was no reason to think the bowman would hesitate to dispatch her when he deemed the time was right.

Again, the memory of Clint's thumb brushing over the old scars on her arm made Natasha pause. What had that meant, that touch? She could have sworn she felt tenderness, or something like it, in his caress. It must have been another strategy, a method for getting under her defenses. She had used such ploys herself, too many times to count. Still, she couldn't help but wonder—was there a chance it had been genuine?

You would be the last woman in the world to recognize an honest emotion. That was the bottom line, really. In the simple calculus of spycraft, she could not afford to let her guard down with this man, or she could wind up with something far worse than a broken heart. Expert marksman he might be, but Clint was perfectly capable of killing at close range.

Natasha stopped and checked her compass. *Chort poderi.* She had wandered off course again. Natasha turned to head in the correct direction when she saw a light, like a firefly's glow, flying toward her. She started running, but it was too dark to see clearly, and she slammed into a tree. Moving more cautiously, she saw another glowing light heading her way, and this time she could hear the distinctive whistle of an arrow arcing through the air.

Hawkeye! Natasha thought quickly about concealing herself, but she felt the impact of the archer's body slamming her down onto the ground before she could move.

"What's wrong, Nat?" he said, pinning her wrists with his hands and immobilizing her legs between the iron clamp of his thighs. "Couldn't sleep?"

The man either had Stark-designed contact lenses to help him navigate the darkness, or else he had the best natural night vision in the world. Natasha struggled for a moment, and then let her muscles go slack, as though realizing she could not match his greater strength. "Sorry, I didn't mean to disturb you when I got up."

"You're too kind."

Natasha reared up, slamming her head into his, and then the two were rolling on the ground, each grappling furiously for the advantage. When they stopped, Natasha had her Glock pressed to Clint's temple, and he had his knife at her throat.

"Stalemate," he said. "I feel you tense, I open your jugular."

"I feel you start to move, I blow your brains out."

It was a perfect stand-off—except they were lying down, pressed up against each other so intimately that Natasha could feel every hard muscle in the bow-man's sinewy body. "You feel like telling me why you snuck out of camp, Nat? Or should I spare you the trouble of lying about going to rejoin Lykos's people?"

"I'm not on Lykos's side—not yet. But joining up with him is looking more attractive by the minute."

"I suppose that's my cue to try to convince you that we're a better bet?" Clint smiled, but his eyes were cold and hard. "Lady, you've got to the count to three to convince *me* I shouldn't just remove you from the equation before you betray our group to Lykos."

"What's the point? You've made up your mind, and there's nothing I can say that will change it."

"One."

Natasha's mind raced, thinking of stratagems, wrestling holds, ruses.

"Two."

She wished she were not so aware of his body on a purely animal level. She wished he hadn't touched her arm so softly back by the campfire.

"Three."

She felt his muscles tense at the same time hers did, and then it happened so quickly that even Natasha wasn't entirely sure who initiated the kiss. All she knew was that his hands were now tangled in her hair, and her nails were digging into his shoulders, and he was kissing her so fiercely it sent sparks down her spine, electrifying every last inch of her. They were grappling again, but this time, anger had been transmuted into something else. Or perhaps it had been something else all along, and the anger had been the disguise. They were not gentle with each other. They were not even gentle with themselves as they rolled on the rough ground, yanking back the clothing that was a barrier to closer contact.

At the last possible moment, Clint hesitated, searching her face. "Natasha. Is this what you want?"

"No," she said, wanting him to understand that she hadn't chosen this, it had chosen her. But as he began to withdraw, she grabbed him and said fiercely, "yes," repeating the word over and over until he took her, returning her ferocity with equal force. He tried to kiss her, and Natasha bit him on the shoulder, hard. This was the furthest thing in the world from the carefully choreographed seduction scenes she had used to manipulate men in the past. It was nothing like what she had shared with Alexei, either. This was something new, as primal and dangerous as their surroundings. With the tiny part of her brain that was still functioning, Natasha knew it would serve her right if she were to be eaten by some stupid reptile.

Then, just as the sensation threatened to overwhelm her, Clint cupped the back of her head, protecting her from the hard ground, and kissed her again, and Natasha stopped thinking altogether.

CLINT tried to recall when he had done anything this stupid. As a kid in the Iowa Lutheran Foundation Group Home, sick of having his meager belongings swiped, when he had dug up a nest of fire ants and dumped them in Erik Gregerson's bed? As a teenager in the circus, when he had gone on stage so drunk he couldn't walk straight, and then attempted a tumbling run? Or perhaps it had been during the start of his brilliant criminal career, when he had tried to shut up a family's golden retriever without hurting it, and had wound up with thirty stitches in his hand and a prison record.

No, thought Clint, as the first rays of dawn filtered down through the leaves, revealing the elegant curve of Natasha's back as she straightened her clothing.

None of that compared in sheer, reckless, damn-the-consequences stupidity to this. He took a deep breath, trying to think what to say, and then realized Natasha had her back to him. *Christ.* She looked over her shoulder, and they both rolled for their weapons at the same moment.

"I feel like we've done this before," he said, his grip steady on his bowstring as he tried not to think what the arrow would do to that pretty face.

"There's a slight variation in position." Natasha indicated the Glock, aimed at his heart instead of his head.

Clint didn't make any wisecracks. It seemed a bit ridiculous to go back to flirty banter when his knees were still weak from their last encounter. "Nat," he said, and then, surprising even himself, continued, "I'm putting down the bow." She simply stared at him, unblinking, as he placed his recurve gently on the ground, and then held up his hands, palms out. "If what just happened here was you playing me, then go ahead and shoot."

Her gun hand didn't waver. "Of course I was playing you, the same as you are playing me now. I must admit, you're very good, to risk it all just to wrangle a little more information."

"Look, I know it's kind of embarrassing, but let's face it. What just happened here—" Clint gestured at the grass, pressed flat by the imprint of their bodies. "You can't tell me that was part of some plan."

"Please. Don't insult my intelligence. You know as well as I do that in our line of business, sex is just another weapon."

Clint considered all the ways women could feign passion. He thought, not for the first time, that Mother Nature had given them one hell of an advantage in the deception department. He thought about how many men had let their egos sway them into thinking that of course she was a master manipulator, but that time with me, hey, that had to be different. He thought about the fact that, as far as he was aware, he and Nat had both left themselves unprotected—in more ways than one.

It was a lot of thinking, but it all took about a second, and then Clint made his decision. "This isn't a movie, Nat. We can't just stand here like this debating things for an hour. You're either going to have to shoot me or put the gun down." He took a step forward.

"Stop right there."

"I'm not stopping." He took another step, and then another. The Glock's muzzle was flush against his chest now.

Her jaw was set. "I don't want to kill you."

"I know," said Clint, his voice softening. "I don't want to kill you, either." It was probably the least romantic thing Clint had ever said to a woman afterwards, but it seemed to have the desired effect.

"Chort poderi!" Natasha lowered the gun, slipping the safety back on. "I can't decide if you're the most brilliant opponent I've ever faced, or a complete mental defective."

"Does it have to be one or the other?" Clint nodded at the gun she was holstering in her belt. "You can keep that."

She cocked an eyebrow at that. "Gee, thanks."

"Look." Clint picked up his bow and wiped a wet leaf off the grip. "I'm not saying that we should just start trusting each other blindly. I think what we should do is declare a temporary truce."

The crease between her eyebrows deepened. "And how would this détente work, precisely?"

"You know where Lykos's camp is, right? Well, you lead me to it and then back to my team, and I'll vouch for you." He watched her as she thought it over. "On the other hand, you take me there and try to sell me out to the bad guys, and I'll have to reevaluate our relationship."

She gave him the briefest of smiles. "You *are* mentally defective."

"Most likely. Is it a deal?" He held out his hand.

Natasha took it. "When a lefty offers you his right hand, what does it mean?"

Clint couldn't resist. "Good point. Want to seal the deal with a kiss?"

"I don't think so," said Natasha, taking her hand back and checking the compass she had stolen from him before setting off in an easterly direction. "You're not very good at this, are you?"

"Oh, so *that's* what all the groaning was about," said Clint, following her lead. "You were trying to complain."

Natasha let a branch swing back, hitting Clint in the forehead. "Sorry. Maybe you should concentrate on where you're going."

"'Cause I kind of thought you were having a seizure."

After that, the path began to ascend steeply, and there was no more breath for talking. But even from the back, Clint could tell that Natasha was smiling.

BY 6 a.m., Clint's entire body was slick with sweat. Natasha had stripped down to her sports bra, but neither of them had thought to grab water before heading out. "Not that I don't admire your stamina," he called out, "but I don't think we should go much farther without locating a water source."

Natasha slicked her hair back from her face. She was so drenched with perspiration, it looked as though she had taken a shower. "Do you have any idea what kind of things we're likely to find around a water source?"

"Yeah, but I thought there was some kind of temporary animal truce when you go drink. At least, that's the way it looked in all the Disney specials."

She gave him a contemptuous look. "It's only a truce until somebody attacks."

"True. But that might be enough time to grab a quick drink." He unwrapped the leather band from around his bow arm. "Hold on a minute."

"What are you doing?"

"Tying your hair back." He wrapped the leather around her shoulder-length hair, pulling it into a sloppy ponytail. "How is that?"

"Better." She looked surprised. Clint wondered whether, for all her experience seducing men, she wasn't used to men making nice gestures. "So," she said brusquely, "what's your plan for locating water?"

"Well, I…" Just as Clint was about to admit that he didn't have a clue, he heard a crack of thunder. "I thought I'd just order room service."

"Very clever." There was a second thunderclap, louder and closer than the first. "Do you think…" Her words were cut off by the rain, which came down in sudden, tropical torrents, drenching them both instantly.

They looked at each other, both laughing at the same time as the rain sheeted down, a heavy curtain separating them from the rest of the world.

"So how do you like my plan?"

"What?"

Giving up on conversation, Clint leaned back, mouth open, and drank. Natasha copied him, and then Clint reached for her hand and ran with her, taking shelter under a large tree. He moved his bow and quiver into a depression in the trunk and pulled off his vest to cover it. He had a small canteen on his belt, but it was empty. He opened it and propped it against a small tree. When he turned back to Natasha, she quickly raised her eyes from his chest. Ah, he thought. *Nice to know.*

"How long do you think this will last?"

"Not sure," he said. "Not too long, I think."

There was a clap of thunder, and then the rain came down even harder, so he could barely hear her response. He'd seen tropical rains before, but never anything like this. He leaned in closer. "What?"

She repeated it, but he shook his head again. "Sorry."

He focused on her mouth, trying to read her lips, and then they were kissing again. He made his way from her neck to her collarbone, which tasted slightly salty, and then he kissed lower and Natasha's hands tangled in his short hair, yanking him up. Startled, Clint looked up into her remarkable green eyes, trying to figure out what the problem was. To his shock, he saw there were tears running down her cheeks.

He cupped her face in his hand, then realized she wasn't crying, that it was a trick of the rain. He kissed her cheeks nevertheless, just to make sure, but then she turned her head and they were mouth to mouth again. Suddenly, Natasha tucked her head into the side of Clint's neck and he felt the vibration in Natasha's chest as she cried out, saying words the rain and the thunder stole before he could make out their meaning. He'd never been a talker before, but Clint found himself saying all manner of crazy things. Confessions. Promises. Declarations.

When it was over, though, Natasha remained in his arms, and Clint found himself kissing the top of her head. You'd think, having made the mistake already, that a second time wouldn't compound anything. But this time felt like a whole different kind of insanity. When the rain let up a bit, Natasha turned her head. "So, have you decided not to kill me yet?"

He tensed, and then forced his muscles to relax. "What do you mean?"

"You're under orders, correct? And you've been trying to decide whether to follow them."

Jesus. Clint turned Natasha in his arms so he could see her face. "What gave it away?"

Natasha smiled, touching his mouth. "You. Right now. But I suspected."

Clint pressed a kiss to the tips of her fingers. "What about you? You made up your mind whether you're going to live up to your namesake?"

She made a throaty little sound of surprise. "Stop that."

He had sucked her fingers into his mouth. "Thtop whath?"

Natasha reclaimed her hand, wiping it on his chest. "You have not been trained in the seduction arts, I take it?"

"Carson's Traveling Carnival did not offer that particular talent, I'm afraid. You?"

"Of course." She settled back against his bare chest, resting her head over his heart. "Couldn't you tell?"

"Um, would you be terribly insulted if I said no? Or is that the point of the seduction arts?"

Natasha didn't say anything for a moment. "How much longer till the storm passes, do you suppose?"

Clint stroked her hair and looked out at the rain. "It's letting up now, so not long."

She pressed her lips to his chest. "I wish it would keep going."

Clint tightened his arms around her until he was sure she was going to protest, but instead she gripped him back just as firmly. Oh, man, he was drowning here. If these were the seduction arts, then he was a goner. Trying to defuse the intensity, he relaxed his hold a little and said, "If you're really set on killing me—can we do it at least one more time first?"

She laughed. "If we keep doing this, we're both going to wind up dead."

Her words were prophetic. There was a sound from the branches overhead, and then they were under attack in a blur of fur and fangs. But not by animals.

Pinning Clint to the ground, Nekra bared her fangs in a vampiric smile and said, "Were you looking for us?"

On his other side, Clint saw Mandrill on top of Natasha, and something in the man's simian features made him tense. "Because we certainly enjoyed looking at you." Then he laughed, wild hoots of baboon laughter that reverberated through the jungle.

THIRTEEN

NEKRA'S corpse-pale face and vampiric fangs were even more shocking out in the jungle sun than they had been under the fluorescent prison lights. "I like the black combat gear," she purred as she raked Clint's face with her long, sharp nails. As Natasha watched, he managed to get her in a leg-lock.

Nekra widened her eyes. "Ooh, big boy," she said, before going for his eyes.

Natasha looked up at Mandrill, thinking furiously. Back in the program, Natasha and Yelena had been forced to memorize the biographies and skill-sets of hundreds of super heroes and villains, the same way medical students might learn the characteristics of various illnesses. Mandrill and Nekra were clearly both preternaturally strong and fast. In any direct hand-to-hand-combat situation, Natasha and Clint were outmatched, which meant they had to be clever.

Unfortunately, Jerome Beechman was an extremely intelligent man underneath the simian physiognomy. Which begged the question: Why was he just sitting on Natasha, instead of beating her up?

"Do you feel it yet?" The furred hand stroked her cheek. "I must admit, I don't usually enjoy other men's...leavings. But you are something special."

Oh, *kakaya merzost.* She had forgotten about his pheromones. Now, that was a big heaping plate of repulsive. Still, it was something she could work with. "Don't touch me, you animal!" She strained against him, thrashing her head for good measure.

"You won't feel that way for long."

"Clint, help, don't let him...don't..." Natasha widened her eyes. "Don't touch me."

"Don't touch you—like this?" He trailed one furred finger down the center of her chest. "Or like this?" Before he could complete the move, Natasha had jammed her knee up into his nose and rolled.

"For a supposedly brilliant scientist, you really are quite stupid," said Natasha, sweeping his legs out from under him with a kick before stomping on his kidney, hard. "Pheromones work subliminally. Keep calling attention to them, and you allow a person to guard against the effect." She grabbed the Glock and turned from the prostrate Mandrill to check on Clint.

"Well done, girlie," snarled Nekra. "But you might want to give yourself up...before I remove your man's eyeball." She had Clint on his knees in a chokehold, and her dagger-sharp fingernail was positioned at the corner of his right eye. Clint looked at Natasha with a familiar, slightly rueful smile.

"Sorry," he said. "Got distracted there."

"So sweet," said Nekra. Her black hair was pulled back so tightly from her skull, it gave Natasha a headache just looking at it. "I might give you his eye as a souvenir."

"What do I care? I was just using him," said Natasha, shrugging. Mandrill was beginning to stir; she didn't have long. "Unlike you, I do not weaken myself with personal attachments."

"Oh, all right, then." Nekra began to press her finger into Clint's eye. "You might not want to watch this part."

"I won't. I'll be too busy shooting your man in the head." Natasha pressed the gun's muzzle at the back Mandrill's skull.

"Idle threat. Avengers don't kill."

"I'm not an Avenger," said Natasha. "I'm not even a super hero. In fact, I don't have any powers. So if I hesitate to kill, it's a pretty fair bet that the super-powered folks will kill me instead." She cocked the gun.

It seemed impossible, but Nekra's face went even paler. "Let him go. Look. I'll give you your man back."

"You first."

"At the same time."

They stared into each other's eyes. Just as Natasha was about to agree, something shifted behind Nekra's flat, dark gaze. "Do you have any idea how much I despise you? With your pretty face, you could go any-where. Do anything." Nekra's hands, clamped around Clint's neck now, trembled with rage. The black leather outfit she wore seemed equal parts bondage gear and Halloween costume, but her expression was pure anguish and fury. "You don't belong here. You belong in the normal world, with normal people, sit-ting at some stupid coffee house drinking macchiatos and planning your career and your nursery and your vacation in Aruba."

I have to snap her out of this, thought Natasha. *But how?* The mutant woman's power was fueled by hate, and she was riding a wave of it now, making her irrational and unpredictable and enormously, dangerously strong.

Suddenly the ground around Nekra began to trem-ble, as if an earthquake were beginning, but this was no shifting of tectonic plates. All around them, small, dead things were clawing their way to the surface. A desiccated tree shrew. The skeletal remains of a small dinosaur. The half-eaten carcass of a young ape, slung up in the branches of a tree by some predator, was painstakingly making its way down to the ground.

Zombies. Nekra was calling up zombies, perhaps not even consciously aware of what she was doing. Thank God there weren't any larger corpses around, thought Natasha.

And then she felt the ground shifting under her feet. There *was* a larger corpse, and it was about to break through. For a moment, Natasha couldn't think what to do. Then it came to her, the pertinent detail from the woman's file: Nekra's power was fueled by rage.

"You think I'm normal?" Natasha forced herself to disregard the dead things encircling them and tried not to think about how long Clint's air supply had been cut off. Instead, she concentrated on Nekra. "You have no idea. Maybe I can pass, like Lykos when he's in his human form, but inside? I'm more a monster than any of you."

Unfortunately, Mandrill had learned his lesson about not announcing his moves all too well. He reared up without warning, seizing Natasha's wrist and forcing her to drop the gun.

But Clint managed to use that moment of surprise to flip Nekra onto her back. Now their positions were reversed, with Clint's knife at Nekra's throat and Mandrill's arm choking Natasha.

"Let's try this again," said Clint. "How about you let the lady go, and I don't turn your girlfriend's black-and-white look all red?"

Mandrill gave a roar of rage.

"Yeah, I know, she pissed you off. But let's just call this one a draw, okay? Count of three?"

Mandrill threw Natasha away from him at the same moment that Clint released Nekra. As Mandrill helped his pale companion to her feet, he snarled at Clint. "You think it's just us you're up against? Lykos is gathering an army. Americans, Russians—you're all the same. You've raped your own land, but you can't have Pangea."

With that, he slung Nekra over his shoulder and

bounded off. The jungle swallowed them up within seconds.

Natasha and Clint looked at each other. "You okay?" He touched her throat.

"What is it with you and the count of three, anyway? What are we, toddlers?"

"I can't believe you nearly let that woman gouge out my eyeball with her talon."

"I can't believe you let her get that close."

"I was watching you and the monkey man!"

"Well, don't. I don't expect you to save me, so don't expect me to save you."

She turned from him, astonished at her own burst of temper. She never got mad. She never lost control. That was the first thing they had taught her in the program.

"Listen, Nat. I don't know how it works where you come from, but if you want to join our little clubhouse, then you ought to know that I will expect you to save me, same as I'd expect it from Jessica or Steve or Luke or Tony. And you should expect the same from us. It's not about the sex. It's about the teamwork."

She whirled to face him. "Your precious Jessica is lying to you, and you're too blind to see it!"

His response was curiously mild. "Maybe. What are you too blind to see, Nat?"

The sat phone at his waist beeped, and Clint picked it up. "Yes, I've located her. We've also encountered two of the escaped inmates." He paused, listening. "Affirmative. We'll start making our way back to camp." He replaced the phone in a holster on his hip.

"What's going on?"

"We've got a location for Lykos. Luke and Peter ID'd him at the citadel, but the place is crawling with locals—mutant Savage Landers."

Natasha frowned. "Interesting."

"They want to rendezvous...I've got the new coordinates. Come on. We've got a lot of ground to cover."

He set off, trusting Natasha to follow him. She looked out at the leafy tangle of trees and vines, thinking how easy it would be to slip away. Clint didn't turn around. A moment before he disappeared from view behind a thick bush, Natasha fell into step behind him.

THE strange, short night seemed to arrive suddenly, so Clint and Natasha stopped to eat and make a small fire. Clint estimated they were only five miles or so from the coordinates Cap had given him. Ordinarily, he would have pressed on, but traversing the jungle required a combination of intense physical effort and supreme vigilance. Fatigue could be as debilitating as alcohol when it came to judgment and reflexes, and he and Natasha were both wiped out enough to make mistakes. Clint noticed Natasha was barely touching the small bird he had caught for their dinner.

"You going to tell me what's bugging you?"

"Your friend Jessica has her powers back."

That would certainly explain how she had beaten Natasha so quickly in their fight. "You sure about that?"

"Positive. Why hasn't she told anyone? Maybe she's working for this rogue S.H.I.E.L.D. outpost. She could be setting us all up."

"Not Jessica."

Natasha pushed her hair back from her face. "Clint, she used to work for Hydra."

"Past tense."

"You really think you can trust her?"

"Funny, she asked the same thing about you." Clint turned the small bird leg in his hands, trying to find a decent bite. "Whatever Jessica's doing, I know she'd never betray her friends." Looking up, he said, "You told Nekra that you were a monster."

"You're changing the subject."

"I've done things I'm not proud of, too. That doesn't make me a monster."

"Clint, no offense, but whatever you've done? Compared to me, you're a choirboy."

Clint looked at her. Even with her face bare of makeup and her hair a tangled mess of waves, she looked sensual, exotic, dangerous. "We comparing how many commandments we've broken? I've taken the name of the Lord in vain about fifty times in the past twenty-four hours. I haven't gone to church since my parents' funeral, and since Dad was a stinking drunk and Mom didn't have the guts to tell him he couldn't drive, I don't honor their memories too much. And just so you don't think I'm handing you a sob story as an excuse, my older brother Barney lived the same life I did, and he joined the Army and then the FBI. As for me, I've lied, I've stolen, I've been coveting other peoples' gear since I could talk."

"Wow. You've convinced me. You're badass." Her voice was as flat as the Iowa plains.

Clint took a breath, and then thought, what the hell. "I've murdered."

"You've killed. There's a difference."

"Nothing wrong with my English, Nat."

They regarded each other through the deepening shadows. When Natasha finally responded, she didn't ask the question he was expecting. Instead, with a voice as soft as a whisper, she said, "How did you lie, Clint?"

It took him a moment, and then he got it. *I take it you have not been trained in the seduction arts.* She had sounded so sophisticated about it, even a bit superior. He, of all people, should have known better than to buy the Mata Hari act. You could call it whatever you liked, but when you manipulated people with your body, there was a certain amount of wear and tear on your soul. "I've lied with my body, if that's what you're asking."

She gave an unladylike snort of laughter. "Please. I'm not talking about some furtive teenage fumbling that you pretend is love for an hour or so."

"Neither am I."

She raised her eyebrows. "S.H.I.E.L.D. asks this of their agents?"

"No. At least, I don't think so." He thought about how much easier this conversation would be if he had a drink. Clint was used to walking into dangerous places, but this was emotional territory he'd sealed off years ago. He'd never talked about it with anybody, not the doctors, not the social workers—not even Jacques Duquesne, who had taken him off the streets and into Carson's Carnival of Traveling Wonders.

Clint picked up a flat stone and passed it between his fingers, an old dexterity exercise he hadn't done in years. "After my parents died, I went to a group home. Then, when I was thirteen, I ran away and spent about three months on the streets. It's not in my file. The group home kept lousy records." He took a drink of water from the canteen, because his mouth was suddenly bone dry. "It was a bad time. I made some bad decisions. Some of them led to bad situations."

"You don't have to say any more. I understand." She stirred the ground with a twig. "Still, it's not the same. You were a child, and desperate. The things I have done…I did as an adult, and nobody forced me." She didn't say anything else.

The silence stretched and became uncomfortable, weighted with unsaid things.

Jesus. Clint stood up to move around, tending the fire, checking the perimeter for predators, anything to keep from meeting her eyes. Of course it wasn't the same. He was a guy, for crying out loud. He had to be out of his mind, admitting his secrets to a woman, to *this* woman. What had he expected her to do, burst into tears, rush over and embrace him, start planning a winter wedding with an archery theme? He was a street kid and she was some kind of master spy, and his sordid past had probably just made her regret ever letting him near her.

"Clint?" Her voice was gentle.

He kept feeding small twigs into the fire. "Yeah."

"We should try to sleep. You want to go first?"

Clint laughed. "And wake up to find you storming the citadel without me? I don't think so."

"Suit yourself." She lay down, pillowing her head on her hands. So much for the easy camaraderie that had gripped them along with the passion. It was for the best, he supposed. Not exactly a great idea to stroll back into camp hand in hand with the notorious Black Widow. And when you came right down to it, he hadn't lost a thing, except maybe one last chance to do the deed. Neither of them was the type for white lace and happily ever afters.

Within moments, Natasha's breathing slowed and her eyelids began to flutter. Not that he was watching or anything. *Wonder what she's dreaming about,* he thought, and then caught himself. *Whatever it is, Barton, it ain't you.*

FOURTEEN

THE moment Jessica saw Clint and Natasha, she knew something had happened. Her first clue was the obvious fact that Clint wasn't dragging the Black Widow back in handcuffs. Instead, they walked in together, his longer legs keeping pace with her smaller strides. His body language was another tell: There was no wariness in the way Clint's eyes followed the Russian agent, but still he kept glancing over at her as she greeted Peter and Luke.

Great. No use talking to him now. He'd just repeat every word to his new handler.

"Hey, Jessica." Clint dropped his quiver and bow at the base of a tree, and crouched down by the first-aid kit. "Are we the last to arrive?" He tore open an alcohol wipe and applied it to a scratch on his face. The Black Widow, Jessica noted, did not appear to have sustained any injuries.

"Steve and Tony are due back anytime now. Everyone else is here."

Clint unzipped his vest and swabbed a scratch on his chest. "What's taking them so long?"

"The usual—bad luck and snafus."

Clint looked up. "We talking snafus with teeth, or some other kind?"

"Steve's had teeth. Tony said he was having some kind of armor glitch." Jessica pointed at the scratches. "Did you get into a fight?" She regretted the question almost instantly. If those were marks of passion, she really didn't want to know.

Clint zipped up his vest. "We ran into Nekra and Mandrill. Hey, is there anything to eat?"

"Luke's making something out of the MRE pouches. I think he's mixing macaroni and cheese with sweet-and-sour pork, so you might want one of these instead." Jessica handed him an energy bar.

"Thanks." He unwrapped the foil and took a bite, examining a topographical map displayed on Jessica's laptop. Small dots indicated each team member's location. Steve's and Tony's dots kept inching closer to the new camp.

"So, what's the report on the S.H.I.E.L.D. outpost?"

"I got called back before I reached it."

Clint looked over his shoulder. "Really? You didn't try to fly there?"

Jessica blinked in surprise, and then recovered. "I think my powers might be coming back, but they're not reliable yet. That's why I haven't said anything yet. How could you tell?"

"I couldn't."

Without another word, Clint walked over to offer some of his energy bar to Natasha. It seemed like the kind of gesture you saw in high-school romances, at least in the movies. Jessica had never been to high school and had accidentally killed her first teenage crush with a power blast.

She had lived with the guilt of that action for years. *And that's the big difference between me and a certain Russian,* she thought. Jessica would bet her life savings that when the Black Widow used her powers to destroy a man, there was nothing accidental about it.

Jessica crossed the camp to where the Russian woman was accepting a cup of Luke's foul-smelling concoction. "Ms. Romanova," she said. "I wonder if we could have a word in private?"

The other woman paused, spoon in hand. "Why in private?"

"It's about shark week."

"All right," she said, putting down her cup. "You lead the way."

Peter paused in the act of pulling off his mask. "I've barely recovered from the monster chickens. Please don't tell me there's some kind of prehistoric land shark about to attack?"

"No, Peter, it's nothing for you to worry about," said Jessica. As she and Natasha moved away from the camp, she could hear Luke chuckling.

"'Shark week' is girl code," he was telling Peter.

"Girl code?"

"Think about it for a sec."

"I still don't…oh. Ugh. Ew. Jeez, Luke, how do you know about it?"

"Pregnancy, man. I know more about women's cycles than I ever dreamed of knowing. You ever hear of a mucus plug?"

Jessica didn't catch Peter's response, but she kept walking until she reached a small copse of trees to be certain she and Natasha would have privacy.

"Okay," said Natasha, "I'm assuming you didn't really drag me out here to ask if I have a box of tampons stashed in my boot. But before you start grilling me, I'd like to know one thing: Are you loyal to S.H.I.E.L.D., or to your friends here?"

"I'm loyal to both. What about you? Are you loyal to anyone besides yourself?"

To Jessica's surprise, Natasha did not respond immediately. Instead, she appeared to consider the question. "Yes," she said, sounding slightly surprised.

Oh, thought Jessica, nice acting. "Go on," she prompted. "Don't stop there. Isn't this where you confess that yeah, you've been seducing men for information since you were thirteen, but this thing with Clint is different?" Jessica brought her hands to her chest and batted her eyelashes.

Natasha nodded, as if acknowledging a point. "And is this where you finally come clean about *your* feelings for Clint?"

Should have seen that one coming. "Clint and I are partners. You think lust is a big indicator of intimacy? I say friendship counts for more than some temporary hormonal high."

"Speaking of hormones, your file mentioned that you have some kind of genetically altered pheromones that attract most men and some women. Kind of like Mandrill. Wonder why they haven't worked on Clint. Could it be that he genuinely likes me?"

"I'm sure he thinks he does."

"I also recall that your scent seems to repel other heterosexual women. Must make it difficult to get along with people at work—half of them want to jump your bones, and the other half want to break them. Guess that's why you're so upset about Clint." Natasha walked a slow circle around Jessica. "He is your only real friend, isn't he?"

"Your information's out of date," said Jessica, refusing to turn her head to follow Natasha's progress. "I have a perfume that neutralizes the effect of my pheromones. Unlike *some* people, I don't intentionally use sex to manipulate my friends."

"Ah, another secret emerges. I am so enjoying our little girl talk."

Damn it. The perfume was new, another gift from Hydra's research-and-development team. This woman was dangerously good at getting information, and Jessica felt the prickle of alarm turn into a shiver of electricity moving down her arms. Without her Spider-Woman powers, she wasn't sure which of them would emerge victorious from a fight. With them, Jessica knew, she could blast the other woman off her feet and out of the game. And, oh, man, did she ever want to zap this manky skank.

Natasha suddenly looked wary, as if she could sense

the shift in Jessica. "I know you won't believe me, but I'm not manipulating Clint."

"Please. It may not even be deliberate, but all you've ever done is manipulate people. You wouldn't know how to be any other way."

Natasha stopped in her tracks. "All right, then, as long as we're digging around in each other's psyches, why don't we talk about *how* you got your powers back?"

This time, Jessica had anticipated Natasha's next move. "They just came back. I didn't want to get anyone's hopes up until I was certain."

"So you won't care if I just announce your happy recovery to everyone?"

The power was thrumming inside Jessica now. "Be my guest."

"I could also suggest to Tony that he scan you for any sign of surgery or enhancements."

Jessica grabbed Natasha and flipped her, then straddled the smaller woman. "What's your game now? Is this some kind of ploy to get Clint to rush in to save you?"

"You know, Clint told me to start treating you like a teammate, but you're making it awfully difficult." Natasha kicked out; before Jessica could react, she found their positions reversed. Now she was on her back, a Glock pointed at her heart.

"I have no idea whether or not I can trust you, Jessica, and I don't have a lot of time to decide. I'm going to take a chance and tell you there are things going on that you don't understand. So before you make your next move, consider this." Natasha leaned in so her mouth was right next to Jessica's ear. "Look up. We're surrounded."

For a moment, Jessica didn't understand. Natasha moved back to allow Jessica to get up. Jessica stared at the Black Widow for a moment, trying to decide whether this was yet another trick. Then she caught a flicker of movement out of her peripheral vision and saw what the other woman had already noticed: shadowy figures crouched in the trees around them—at least a dozen, maybe more.

If there had been time, Jessica would have been furious at herself for letting down her guard. She tried not to worry about Clint and the others back at the camp. She had to keep herself grounded in the here and now. *If I survive this, I'm going to owe Natasha.*

"So," she said to Natasha, "are we going to yammer on about it all day, or get down to it?"

"Let's do it." Natasha pulled Jessica up.

The two women stood back to back, facing their misshapen attackers. God, they were huge—densely muscled, and armed with claws and fangs. From the looks of their blunt faces, three of the mutates had been gorillas in a former life. The other two looked like they had been some kind of felines: lions, perhaps, or tigers.

"Oh, great, cats," Natasha said, not looking away from the mutates.

"You don't like cats?"

"I'm allergic, so they always go for me."

The cat-mutates pounced, all three coming at Natasha at once. "What did I tell you?" Natasha pushed at the shortest one's chin—giving it a hard, lateral shove—and then she darted sideways, causing the three mutates to crash into one another. They recovered almost instantly, but Natasha was already delivering a roundhouse kick that toppled her attackers like bowling pins.

Jessica didn't see what happened next because she was busy with the two ape-mutates. They hauled their fists back to deliver twin knockout punches to her jaw, then hollered in pain as Jessica ducked under their arms, causing them to punch each other. Jessica delivered a sharp double-handed blow to her attackers' unprotected groins, and the two grunted in unison.

"You guys aren't much for the fighty conversation, are you?" Out of the corner of her eye, Jessica saw a cat-mutate flip Natasha onto her back. Natasha grabbed a fistful of her opponent's fur and gave it a ferocious yank. The cat-mutate let out a yowl of pain. He stumbled back, staggering into the other two, dazed mutates. They exchanged a quick glance and fled, back into the trees.

"I'm going to pay for this with a wicked rash," said Natasha, blowing the fur from her palms.

"Come on, let's get back to the others." Jessica raced ahead—and then stopped, stunned. Clint, Luke and Peter lay sprawled on the ground.

"Clint!" She crouched down beside him, trying to find a pulse. His bow was still in his hand. Whatever had taken him down must have hit him fast. There was no mark on him.

"Is he dead?"

"No, there's a pulse. It's weak, but it's there. And he's breathing." She checked Peter while Natasha pressed two fingers to the radial artery in Luke's wrist, and then the larger carotid artery at his neck.

"Unconscious, but breathing," said Natasha.

"Same with Peter." Jessica lifted one of his eyelids, then slapped him lightly on the cheek. "Well, his pupils are responding, but he's not."

"What could have gotten to them like this?" Jessica pulled out her sat phone. "Tony, Steve, can you hear me?" She felt a hand on her shoulder and paused. "What?"

"Over there." Natasha pointed and then Jessica saw them: Steve and Tony, lying on the ground, their bright costumes partially hidden by the long grass.

Jessica pressed her head to Steve's chest. "The same as the others. How is Tony?"

"Who can tell, under all this armor?" Natasha sat back on her heels. "What mutant is powerful enough to overpower all of them?"

"God, I don't know. What do we do? Give them adrenaline? I've got some basic first-aid training, but that's all."

She began to get up, but Natasha grabbed her arm. "Wait!"

Three new mutates emerged from behind the treeline. One was a skinny little man with weasel-sharp eyes set far below an enormous bald head. The second was a four-handed giant, and the third a blue-skinned blonde with red geometric patterns on her arms and legs. She raised her arms, and Jessica was frozen. Jessica glanced at Natasha: The Russian woman was also struggling in the grip of an unseen, paralyzing force. The blue-skinned blonde must have some kind of powerful telekinetic ability.

Then there was the leathery sound of immense wings, and a pteranodon landed in the clearing. It was an astonishing sight—nine or ten feet tall, covered with thick, pebbled orange skin, with a crested skull and a long, wickedly sharp beak. Most astonishing of all was the creature's eyes—large, golden and filled with an uncanny intelligence. As she gazed into those cruel, clever eyes, Jessica thought: This was no mere reptile. This was something else, something more.

"What are you?" Jessica did not know whether she spoke the words or merely thought them.

"Sauron," said the creature. "Now, sleep." The tone of its voice, the timbre, compelled obedience.

Jessica felt herself falling, but the ground didn't seem to be where it ought to have been. She felt as if she were falling for a very long time, and then she felt nothing at all.

FIFTEEN

JESSICA woke up with the kind of headache usually preceded by a bottle of tequila, hours of sitting next to speakers and a lot of secondhand smoke. The pulsating pain in the back of her head wasn't her only problem, though. Her wrists and shoulders ached with a steady, hot burn that came from seriously overworked muscles. She realized she was hanging by her arms, although there was something around her waist that kept some of her weight off her wrists. Jessica blinked, trying to get a sense of her surroundings, and abruptly realized two things: One, she was hanging alongside her teammates, in a circle. And two...

"Yep," said Peter. "We're naked."

"Oh, my God," she said, not knowing where to look. She couldn't see anything holding them up, which meant there was some sort of force field around their wrists and waists. Unfortunately, the force field was completely invisible, which meant nobody was keeping any secrets now. There was Steve, still unconscious, his pale body as perfect as a Michelangelo sculpture without his red-white-and-blue Captain America suit. Next to him was Natasha, and next to her…Jessica caught Clint's rueful look, and she felt her face flush. She averted her gaze, only to get an eyeful of Peter's lanky, gymnast's form. She saw a flash of Tony's sinewy arms and furred chest and turned away, only to find herself confronted by Luke Cage's big barrel chest and tree-trunk thighs. "They couldn't have just left us with underwear?"

"That wouldn't have helped, in my case," said Peter.

Jessica stared at him, startled. "You're telling me you don't wear underwear?"

"The suit has a built-in liner. And don't look so disgusted. At least I'm not naked during shark week."

Jessica stared at him a moment, and then said, "It's not really—oh, never mind."

"You're blowing it, man," said Luke. "You got to stay cool about the lady stuff."

Jessica rolled her eyes. "Haven't you ever seen a naked woman before?"

"Speaking for myself," said Tony, "I could handle plain old nakedness, but add the frisson of danger…"

Clint said something to Natasha that Jessica could not hear. Natasha looked exasperated and blew a strand of hair out of her mouth. *"Kretinyi."*

For once, Jessica was in complete agreement.

"So," said Clint, "rapidly changing the subject. Anyone know where we are?"

"Yeah," said Tony. "The citadel."

Looking around, Jessica could see that the room was made almost entirely of smooth, silvery metal. Some of the pipes and connections were broken, their edges rough and burnt, while a tattered metallic-mesh fabric hung over a gaping hole where there had once been a window. A warm, amber light filtered in from the outside, giving Jessica some clue as to how much time had passed: hours. There was a spectacular view of the craggy Mountains of Eternity beyond the citadel, and Jessica tried not to think too hard about whether her captors intended to keep her alive long enough to catch the sunrise.

Steve made a strangled sound, his head jerking back. "What the heck…"

"Naked. The citadel. Peter goes commando under his Spidey suit. You haven't missed much," said Jessica. She expected the World War II veteran to be flustered by her nudity, but Steve surprised her by looking her straight in the eyes.

"Typical strategy for psychologically weakening prisoners. Resist it."

"Yes, sir," she said, meaning it.

"None of Lykos's lieutenants have asked any questions yet?"

"Not yet," said Luke. "Yo! Freak squad! Time to come out and explain the big, dastardly plan!"

"Ah. You are finally all awake. Good." The voice was high and nasal and disturbingly munchkin-like.

But the man who emerged from the shadows was only middling short, perhaps five feet tall or so, and extremely thin. "I was beginning to think we had damaged the good Captain, and might not be able to use him in our experiments." Like the aliens in old *Star Trek* episodes, the man's bald head was enormous and slightly egg-shaped; his silver diadem, trim goatee, sheepskin vest, tight breeches and lace-up hippie boots suggested that he was deliberately cultivating a retro-sci-fi look.

"Brainchild," said Tony. "I'd like to know how you got me out of my armor without blowing yourself up." Tony's red-and-gold Iron Man suit was spread out on a long, low table along with a screwdriver, a turning fork, a scrolling wrench and a portable band saw.

"I must admit, I was a little disappointed when I picked the secret out of your mind," said Brainchild, stroking his goatee. "It was really only a mid-week level of crossword complexity. Still, given your limited brain capacity, I suppose one cannot hope for too much."

There was a belch of laughter from behind Brainchild. An enormous, froglike creature appeared, its webbed fingers stroking the gussets on its metal armor. "Off-landers," it croaked, "you have no idea how ridiculousss you look. Ridiculousss...and vulnerable." It fixed its bulbous eyes on Luke; its long, prehensile tongue darted out, making contact with his cheek.

"You try that again," said Luke, "I'm going to bite it off."

"Now, that's a whole new fairy tale," said Peter.

"Leave them alone, Amphibius." Brainchild snapped on a pair of latex gloves. "We discussed the difficulty of maintaining proper hygiene under these trying circumstances."

"I have an allergy to latex," said Tony, warily eyeing the bulbous-headed man as he laid out a number of medical supplies: syringes, catheters, a packet of antiseptic wipes.

"Just so you know," said Luke, "I puke whenever anyone gets near me with a needle. I even puke when someone gets near my wife with a needle. In fact, just seeing that needle, I may puke."

"Oh, don't worry, Mr. Cage, Mr. Stark." Brainchild moved closer to Jessica and Peter. "I have no interest in either of you. You're nothing special."

Tony raised his eyebrows, clearly affronted. "I beg your pardon."

Luke shook his head. "You really want to win *this* argument, Tony?"

"I speak medically, of course. I do have plans for all of you, but I want to start with those who already have profound alterations in their DNA."

Brainchild moved closer to Jessica and Peter, and Jessica felt an old fear slide through her veins. Her father, so familiar in his white labcoat, coming toward her with the syringe. *We need to do this, Jessica, to make you feel better.* She closed her eyes, willing herself not to panic.

"Now, where to begin?" Jessica opened her eyes again as Brainchild ran a hand over Peter's bruised chest. "One, bitten by an irradiated spider during adolescence; the other, infected in utero. So similar, yet so different." He moved to stand directly in front of her.

"Keep your filthy hands off of them," said Steve. "You want to experiment on someone? Start with me."

"Patience, Captain. Your turn will come. But for now…I think the girl, to start." Brainchild went over to a console and flipped a series of switches, and Jessica suddenly felt herself tilting backward. She cried out in surprise, and then found herself lying supine in midair instead of dangling by her wrists. Brainchild flipped another switch, and Jessica's arms moved down to her sides.

Oh, God. This is bad. Icy fear rushed through her, raising goose bumps. "What are you going to do to me?" She hated how high and breathy her voice sounded.

Clint made an odd sound, and Jessica noticed he was straining against the magnetic restraints. "Listen, you bobble-headed squint—you try anything with her, I'm going to smash your oversized cranium like an overripe tomato."

"No need to work yourself into a state," said Brainchild, applying a tourniquet to Jessica's left arm. "My interest in the lovely lady is purely scientific. See?" He draped a blue plastic sheet over her body. "At the moment, I am simply taking a small blood sample." Jessica smelled the familiar, medicinal scent of a Chloraprep swab as Brainchild began rubbing the antiseptic lightly over her inner arm.

"Oh, jeez," said Luke. There was a thin sheen of sweat on his forehead, and Jessica realized he hadn't been lying about his aversion to needles.

"Hey. You. Chihuahua face. You want a body to poke around with?" Clint narrowed his eyes. "Take mine."

Jessica looked over at her partner, touched by his attempt to divert the man's attention and all too aware what he was doing was utterly futile.

"Why should I? According to Lykos, you're nothing but a grunt with a fondness for primitive weapons technology." Brainchild was ripping open the package with the extension tubing now.

"I know this may come as a shock, Humpty, but top-secret medical experiments don't make it into official files. Director Fury's the only one who knows about my surgeries."

Jessica stared at Clint, trying to process this.

"What nonsense." Brainchild attached the syringe to the extension tubing, and then pointed the needle upwards as he depressed the plunger. "You're trying to tell me that S.H.I.E.L.D. kept in-house surgeries so secret that there are no records?"

"They weren't in-house," said Clint, his eyes on Jessica. "I was posing as a double agent to take advantage of Hydra's new medical program. You want to see altered DNA? Come check out mine."

Jessica felt tears well up, clouding her vision. She didn't know how long Clint could continue bluffing a mind-reader; right now Brainchild was distracted. But even if Clint's ploy to save her failed, it didn't matter. All she could think was: *He knows my secret, and he doesn't care.* She had no idea how or when he had discovered she was working with Fury—but he knew, and he understood. "Thank you," she mouthed, knowing he would see it, the way he seemed to see everything.

"Well, well. Perhaps I will attend to you...next." Brainchild tapped Jessica's arm just below the inside of her elbow. "But for now, I'm staying focused on the spider-girl."

"Spider-Woman," said Jessica.

"Ah, forgive me. It was all girl power the last time I saw the news from the surface world."

Brainchild abruptly jabbed the needle into Jessica's arm. He had to make three more attempts before hitting a vein, and Jessica could hear Luke gasp and then slump.

"Jeez," said Tony. "I think he fainted."

"It's not my fault," whined Brainchild. "I'm not a nurse. I'm a research scientist."

"How's your arm, Jess?" The sound of Clint's voice helped Jessica collect herself.

"Sore. But I've had worse." Jessica found herself flashing back to her childhood again—her father coming at her with another, larger hypodermic needle. *Honey, I know you just had a shot, but that one didn't work. We need to try again.* Even now, Jessica could recall the dull ache as the large needle pressed into the small of her back, hitting the bone, and the seemingly endless wait as thick, viscous fluid was depressed from the plunger.

From across the room, Clint was keeping his eyes

on her as though he could rescue her by force of will.

Brainchild was flushing her vein now. As the cool saline spread up her leg, Jessica felt bile rise in the back of her throat. Maybe I should throw up on him, she thought. *Buy myself a little time.*

"I heard that," said Brainchild, stepping away. "Telepathic, remember?"

"Well, hear this," said Peter, his eyes boring into Brainchild's.

Brainchild gave a little billy-goat laugh. "Extremely graphic, but a bit hard for me to imagine, considering your current predicament."

"You're not in charge here," snarled Steve, startling Jessica. "I want to speak to Karl Lykos. Now!" His barked command made Jessica feel less like a frightened prisoner and more like a soldier.

"So speak."

Karl Lykos emerged, lean and handsome and bare chested in his human form, wearing a pair of billowy white trousers and a barbaric-looking metal belt. His eyes, Crusader blue in his swarthy face, regarded the prisoners with clinical detachment. "I'm listening."

"One word," said Steve. "Surrender." He said it with such sharp authority that for a moment, Jessica believed he had some trick up his sleeve.

There was laughter from the back of the room, and now Jessica could see the other mutates gathered there. Barbarus, a great hulking giant of a man, his four arms crossed over his enormous chest; Whiteout, a sylphlike woman dressed all in white, her face obscured by a peaked hood; Lupo, a blue-furred werewolf, crouched on the floor; and Vertigo, her naked blue body patterned with snakelike red-and-blue geometric shapes.

"Maybe I should ask the questions, instead," said Lykos. "What brings you costumes all the way out to the Savage Land? Think carefully before you respond, as my colleague here has methods to elicit the truth."

Was there a drug inside the IV? Jessica wondered. *Please, don't let them drug me.*

"I say we kill them now," said Lupo, his muzzle wrinkled in a snarl.

"But autopsies are so inconclusive," said Brainchild. "I prefer to keep my subjects alive...and conscious."

"Enough," said Lykos, with a disapproving glance at Jessica's prone figure. "There will be no experimentation. That's what *they* do."

"Exactly," said Brainchild. "If we are to defeat our enemies, we don't have the luxury of remaining perched on the moral high ground. We need to discover if you can feed off these subjects, so we can spare our mutates for the real fighting."

"I said no."

"But you don't tell us what to do, Lykos. Do you?" Brainchild stood in front of Jessica, as if protecting her. "Don't forget who brought you here, and for what reason. We don't need your Ph.D. in genetics right now—we need your power as Sauron. And for that, you must feed." He indicated Jessica. "She is not a mutate, but her DNA was altered in the womb. With a little preparation, I think you can feed on this subject."

Lykos drains mutant energies in order to transform

himself into a pteranodon, Jessica thought, suddenly comprehending what Brainchild was saying. But unlike Steve and Luke, whose powers were the results of scientific experimentation, she and Peter had altered DNA. If Lykos could feed off them, he could turn into Sauron without sacrificing any mutates.

But whom are they fighting? There was something far more complicated than a simple prison break going on here.

"Is this what you've become, Karl?" Steve was hanging naked in front of the other man, but it was Lykos's who seemed embarrassed. "You're a doctor. You've taken oaths. More than that, you may have broken laws, but you've always followed your own moral code. Why are you doing this?"

Something flared in Lykos's cold blue eyes. "*I* didn't hunt you down, Captain America. You hunted me. Seems a bit strange to lecture me about moral codes when you would have no compunction about locking me away."

"You broke out of prison, causing the deaths of S.H.I.E.L.D. agents and releasing forty-two dangerous criminals into the general public. What did you expect us to do, let you retire to the Savage Land?"

"I'm not here to retire," said Lykos. "I'm here to fight. And anyone who works with S.H.I.E.L.D. is my enemy."

"Then you ought to let me go," said Natasha. "I'm not with these people. Do you remember, back at the prison? I was there for questioning, at the business end of a gun."

Lykos rubbed his temples. "Were you, really? Why did you come here, then?"

Natasha lifted her chin. "It's a long story. If you let me down…"

"I don't have time for long stories. And frankly, neither do you."

"All right, then," said Natasha. "You want the short version? I'm the Black Widow, the top operative from a very elite school of Russian espionage. As good as I am, I didn't realize that I was being lied to, manipulated…used. I began to investigate, and the trail led to S.H.I.E.L.D.—and then to this place."

"I see," said Lykos. "So these people mean nothing to you, except as a means to an end?" He gestured at Clint and Jessica and the others.

"They are sources of information, nothing more."

"Interesting." Lykos approached Natasha. "And yet Nekra and Mandrill said that you seemed very… chummy with the archer."

The Russian's expression did not waver. "He was under orders to kill me. I had to either turn him or neutralize him. I opted for the former."

Out of the corner of her eye, Jessica watched Clint's face. If you didn't know him well, you might think he hadn't reacted at all to Natasha's betrayal. But Jessica knew him well.

Lykos stepped even closer to Natasha, and Jessica noticed he seemed utterly unaffected by her state of undress. "So you mean to tell me that you have no loyalty to anyone besides yourself?"

"That's right. Free me and I'll fight for you." There

was utter conviction in Natasha's voice. For once, Jessica was convinced the woman was telling the truth.

Lykos sighed. "I do wish I could take you up on your offer. Unfortunately, I cannot afford to risk our mission's safety on an unknown quantity with no particular fondness for our people or our cause." Lykos rubbed his temples again.

He looks tired, thought Jessica.

"Lykos!" A new mutate had entered the room, this one clearly related to a gorilla. Badly injured, the mutate leaned against the door for support. "A group of us are being forced down into an old section of the mines. They want us to see how much damage there is, but one of the mole mutates is certain the whole section is about to collapse. You have to come help."

"Of course." Lykos gripped the gorilla mutate by the shoulder. "Tell me exactly where they are."

"Lykos, you can't!" Brainchild scurried after the taller man like an agitated terrier. "I haven't had time to prepare more serum! And what can you do when you get there? You're too weak to shift!"

"Then give me another injection to tide me over, Brainchild."

"We'll have to make more," Brainchild explained as he prepared a hypodermic with a luminous green fluid.

"Hang on a sec," said Steve. "Are you saying that there's some kind of forced-labor camp in the Vibranium mines?"

"Ah, what innocence. As if there's no blood on your hands."

"Are you saying—S.H.I.E.L.D. would never authorize that kind of a program!"

Lykos smiled without humor as Brainchild injected the hypodermic into his upper arm. "Any government that authorizes the Weapon X program is capable of anything."

Steve frowned. "What's the Weapon X program got to do with this?"

A muscle in Lykos's jaw jumped. "What's your level of security clearance, Captain? Seven? Eight? Higher? You know very well what S.H.I.E.L.D. does behind closed doors."

"You're right, Lykos. I *should* know. Which means that if any of what you're telling me is true, then it is wrong and illegal and I'll bet my life that it's a rogue operation."

"You may be willing to bet your life," said Lykos, "but I'm not willing to bet the lives of any more Savage Landers."

"But that's just what you're doing!" Jessica had never heard Steve sound so heated. "What do you think S.H.I.E.L.D. will do if you marshal a force of mutates to attack its outpost?"

"Oh, I don't know, Captain America," said Brainchild, throwing away the sharps from the hypodermic. "Maybe they'll be too busy attacking the new Mutate Avengers to bother with us."

"Oh, hell, you're going to try to turn me into a giant spider, aren't you?"

"Be quiet," Lykos told Peter. "Brainchild, I did *not* sign off on that." Lykos closed his eyes, and a vein pulsed in his forehead.

Whatever had been in that shot, Jessica thought, it was taking effect.

"Your genetics background would be helpful, but not necessary," said Brainchild. "We have the technology to mutate them, and the manpower. Although I must say, I am a bit disappointed, given all the trouble we went to, breaking you out and bringing you over."

"We're not going to sink to their level," said Lykos. He opened his eyes, revealing the changed color of his irises, the altered shape of his pupils. *He's shifting,* thought Jessica, and she felt her heartbeat increase.

"Besides," Lykos continued, "if any word of this leaks out, there's not enough Vibranium in the world to assure our safety." Gripping the counter with white knuckles, he turned to the other mutates gathered behind him. "Iron Man and Captain America are valuable players. We're better off washing our hands of the whole business." He paused, face contorting in pain.

"Look at his skin," said Luke.

"Barbaros." Lykos's voice was a rasp now.

The four-armed mutate stepped forward. "Yes, doctor?"

"I trust you to perform a clean kill and disposal."

It was over. Jessica glanced up at her friends, trying to think of a way to fight back. *If this were a movie, they'd release us and take us outside first, and we'd have a chance.* But it wasn't a movie.

Barbaros stepped forward with straight razors in two of his four hands.

"I can do clean," he said. "I just need a bucket for the blood."

"What do you think, Steve?" said Tony. "Heard enough?"

"More than enough."

"All right, then...assemble!"

Peter looked as confused as Jessica felt. "Um...Tony? We're all here."

"Not you," said Tony, with no trace of his usual cheerful lechery. Brainchild gave a startled shout as, on the table below, the Iron Man helmet powered up, emitting a blindingly bright beam of light from its eyes.

SIXTEEN

"VOICE command authenticated," the Iron Man helmet said in a bland, robotic voice. The red chest armor rotated on the table next to it, then locked into position under the helmet. "Good evening, Mister Stark."

"Not yet," said Tony, "but it's looking up. Initiate battle mode."

"Battle mode initiated."

"Oh, sweet Christmas, yes!" shouted Luke. Peter hollered his approval as Lykos and Brainchild shouted orders at the other mutates. The Iron Man armor's shoulder pieces assembled themselves, red-and-gold metal sections whirring and clicking and sliding together as if by magic. It only took a matter of seconds for the suit to reconfigure itself, and then the top half was hovering in midair, a repulsor ray holding the mutates to the right of it at bay, while it aimed a high-powered laser at the mutates on the left.

"That's what I'm talking about," said Luke.

"Any chance we can get out of these restraints?" Clint didn't like trusting so many potential threats to one defense.

"Keep your panties on. I'm working on it," said Tony. "Combat orientation, multiple targets. Attack sequence 8, 17, 12, 12, 59 to disarm control panel, unlock access code Pirate Jenny."

There was a blast of light and heat. Brainchild flinched away as the control panel exploded. Clint slammed to the ground, released from his magnetic shackles, and his teammates fell beside him. Natasha landed partially on top of him, and Clint shoved her aside to grapple with the blue-furred Lupo. Rolling to avoid a powerful swipe of the werewolf's sharp claws, Clint sprang up and delivered a roundhouse kick to Lupo's kidney.

Turning, Clint saw Jessica aiming electric venom blasts at the cringing Amphibius. Natasha slammed the heel of her right hand into Whiteout's jaw, knocking off the woman's white-cowled hat. Without missing a beat, Natasha whirled, grabbed Vertigo by one hand and flipped the blue-skinned blonde onto her back. Steve and Luke were facing off against two mutates that looked like Neanderthals with scales, while Tony slammed his fist into Lykos's stomach. The only team member not doing so well was Peter, who was taking a series of punches from Barbaros's four fists.

"What are you waiting for, Lykos?" Cringing under the table, Brainchild's voice rose to a comical screech. "Change!"

"The serum...it's not enough," said Lykos, clutching his stomach and grimacing as his muscles knotted and twisted, creating odd bulges and angles. He lurched toward the open window. "Sorry, Barbaros, but I cannot allow myself to be captured."

Barbaros looked stunned, and he paused with his fist pulled back to punch Peter again. "But, Karl, I thought the Weapon X experiments had—"

Peter's scissor kick to his jaw cut off the rest of his sentence, and Barbaros crumpled to the floor.

"Vertigo, you dizzy blonde," snarled Lupo, still clutching his midsection. "Stop trying to wrestle the redhead. Concentrate! Use your power!"

Out of the corner of his eye, Clint saw the blue-skinned blonde's eyes begin to whirl like some kind of psychedelic light show. Almost instantly, he felt his head grow light, and the room began to spin.

"Tony," said Steve, "you have to end this."

"All right," said Tony. "Everyone, look out. Code Jekyll Cobra Six."

The Iron Man suit blasted a hole in the one remaining wall of the citadel's laboratory, and then fired again, scattering Amphibius and Barbaros and the other mutates into the surrounding jungle.

And just like that, the Avengers were free. Clint raked his hands through his hair, shaking off the bits of dust and debris from the blast. He heard a shrill cry and glanced up at the sky, where two pteranadons were circling. Their bony, sharply crested heads and enormous batlike wings made for a surreal picture against the rising sun. Clint didn't think either of the hungry flying reptiles was Lykos, although he couldn't tell for sure.

"Hoo-aaaah," shouted Luke. "That was righteous. You remember that movie where that *Lord of the Rings* guy goes into a Russian bathhouse and fights two armed guys in his birthday suit?"

"*Eastern Promises*," said Natasha, smiling.

"Well, that guy's got nothing on us."

Steve grinned at Tony. "Stark, you crazy son of a gun, you did it!"

"Yeah, well, I don't think we've got much time to celebrate," said Tony. "Armor, reassemble." The bottom half of the Iron Man suit came hurtling toward Tony. The top half, which had been hovering in midair, flew apart and attached itself to Tony's torso.

Clint found Jessica dressed and pulling on her left boot. "You all right?"

"Yeah. Thanks for trying to cover for me in there. I'm sorry I couldn't tell you before." She looked down, and her dark hair swung forward, concealing her face. "It sounds like you figured out most of it on your own, though."

"How long have you been working for Fury?"

"Since he left. I can't say any more about it."

"Not even to me?"

Clint turned. He had been so engrossed in his conversation with Jessica, he hadn't noticed that Captain America had joined them. Steve had found his costume but not his mask, and the rising sun gilded his fair hair.

Jessica took a deep breath. "Not even to you. I'm sorry, Cap."

"Not as sorry as I am. You can't be a part of this team and keep those kind of secrets." Captain America sounded disappointed rather than angry, but Clint thought she might have preferred his anger.

"Listen, Cap," she said. All the others had drawn closer to hear this exchange. "What Clint said in there was all true—except it wasn't Clint who had the experimental surgery from Hydra. It was me. I've been working undercover for Director Fury."

Tony narrowed his eyes. "So your powers *have* returned? That's what Natasha kept saying. Of course, we didn't believe her, because you claimed *she* was a double agent. Seems you two have more in common than we realized."

Steve turned to Clint. "I'm assuming you knew about this."

"He didn't know! He guessed. Or Natasha guessed and he started to believe her."

Luke folded his arms over his chest. "So the idea is you're working for Fury and not Hydra. I don't suppose you have proof of this?"

Jessica shook her head. "Not until Fury contacts me."

"Until then, you're on probation," said Steve. "I'd tell you to just go home, but that's not an option considering where we are and what's going on."

"I understand, sir. In your place, I'd probably do the same thing."

"I say let her walk home," said Luke. "Lady, you need to decide which side you're on."

Jessica put her hands on her hips. "I shouldn't have to choose between the Avengers and Nick Fury. We all work for Fury."

"With," Tony corrected her. "We work *with* Fury." Tony tapped his finger against his chin. "And it's a relationship that works best when based on a healthy amount of mutual distrust. Armor? Relaunch file-unlock combination for Lykos, Karl. I want to see what S.H.I.E.L.D.'s keeping squirreled away in there. Add Nekra and Mandrill into the mix, while you're at it."

"But I've already exhausted all the standard algorithms," said the helmet, with a trace of a whine in its robotic voice.

"So go a little crazy."

"Define crazy," replied the helmet.

"Oh, I don't know. Randomly permute the variables using an adaptive genetic factor. Try gray coding the thing to prevent premature convergence. Implement Strassen's algorithm for matrix multiplication while using a linear-time Find-Max-Subarray crossing procedure."

The helmet began to talk softly to itself. "Yes, yes, that could work...no, that's not even logical...wait, I see, if the quadrants intersect..." Then it broke off and began to hum tunelessly as it calculated.

"Now, we need to figure out a chain of command," said Steve. "Anyone have any problem following my orders?" He looked at Tony.

"Depends on the orders."

"Well, first off, we have to try to recapture Lykos and the other escaped convicts. It sounds as though they're involved in some kind of conflict situation over by the Vibranium mines, so I suggest we bring the fight to them instead of waiting for them to attack us here."

"And there I have to disagree," said Tony. "I think it's time for us to pay a visit to our local S.H.I.E.L.D. outpost."

Steve looked surprised. "Are you honestly going to take Lykos's word for anything?"

"You don't think it's a bit suspicious that Lykos's Raft files are locked up tighter than Maid Marian's chastity belt?"

"What I think is that S.H.I.E.L.D. is a peacekeeping force," said Steve. "They don't make business deals with foreign powers, they don't get involved with international mining operations, and—above all—they don't experiment on prisoners. Besides, the Savage Land is an internationally recognized world ecological heritage site. It's off-limits to all countries."

Tony placed his helmet on his head, visor up. "I'm glad you cleared that up, Steve. But since S.H.I.E.L.D. doesn't sign my paychecks, I'm inclined to verify my own blind assumptions."

"He does have a point, Cap," said Clint. "It's pretty damn peculiar that the S.H.I.E.L.D. base went radio silent. Either they're under attack, or there's some kind of emergency situation there…"

"Or," said Natasha, "they're up to something that they don't want to advertise to the rest of your organization. I say, check out the S.H.I.E.L.D. base first."

"You don't get a say in this," said Clint.

Natasha looked surprised. "Is this about what happened in there? I thought you, of all people, would figure out what I was trying to do."

Clint picked up his recurve and quiver. "Sounded to me like you were trying to save your ass."

Natasha didn't flinch. "And yet you seem to have no trouble giving Jessica the benefit of the doubt."

"I'm not giving her the benefit of anything. Fury is going to call at some point, and either he'll verify her story or we'll know that she was lying. There's no way anyone can ever know when *you're* telling the truth."

Jessica looked as though he had slapped her. "Excuse me, but why did you defend me in there if you thought I might be working for Hydra?"

Jesus. This was the reason Clint didn't like mixing work and emotions. "It's not black and white, Jess. Whatever you may have done, I don't want to see you getting badly hurt—or killed."

Jessica rounded on him. "So you *still* think I might be working for Hydra?"

Steve stepped between them. "Look, we don't have time to sort through all of this right now."

"All right, then," said Tony. "I say we divide into two groups. Who's coming with me to check out the S.H.I.E.L.D. outpost?"

"I will," said Natasha, instantly going over to his side.

"I'm coming, too," said Jessica, shooting Clint a look. *Well, that makes my decision easy,* thought Clint. "I'll go with Steve to the mines," he said, picking up his quiver and bow. "Who else is coming?"

"If there's slave labor going on, I want to know about it," said Luke.

"I guess I'd better tag along to take care of you." Peter fell into step beside the bigger man.

"Good. There's a small lake by the base of Mount Eternity. We can rendezvous there," Steve told Tony.

They headed off in opposite directions. The New Avengers may have just won their first small victory back at the citadel, Clint thought, but they sure didn't feel like a team.

SEVENTEEN

THE best thing about setting off on a mission with only guys, thought Clint, was that men didn't feel the need to fill the silence with talk. You could just lose yourself in walking and hacking at vines and thinking about how few arrows you had left in your quiver. You could worry about the ways some of the branches shook, testifying to the weight of some unseen creature hunkered down there. You could notice the unsettling fact that you hadn't run into any more terror birds or dinosaurs or mutates, even though they were most certainly out there—watching you, deciding whether you were worth the trouble of killing. With all this weighing on your mind, you didn't have to go digging around in your unconscious or trying to talk about your emotions.

"So," said Peter, "what's the deal with you and Natasha?"

Clint looked at him, then away. "Not a damn thing."

"Seemed like a thing to me."

"Well, it's not."

"What about Jessica?"

"There's nothing going on, okay?"

"Don't need to be so grouchy about it," said Peter, falling back to walk next to Luke. Clint overheard Peter saying, "I got nothing."

Clint stopped and checked his compass. They should be within a mile of the mines, now, but the trees were so thick here it was impossible to see what lay ahead. "You'd think the ground would have cleared out a bit by now, if there'd been mining here."

"Yeah, and if there's activity, we should hear something," said Steve.

Clint held out the compass. "Hold up, let me check our bearings. The needle's acting up."

"Vibranium messes up compasses," said Peter. "At least, large amounts of it do. So if the compass is wonky, it's probably a clue there's a mine-load of the stuff up ahead."

Luke wiped the sweat off his forehead. "That's a relief."

Steve used the side of his shield to hack off a vine as thick as a man's thigh. "Come on, we need to keep pressing on."

They moved with agonizing slowness through the heavy undergrowth. The musky smell of damp vegetation and overripe fruit mingled with the odor of profusely sweating men. The trees had just begun to thin, revealing a patch of blue sky, when Steve stopped abruptly. "Wait. Do you hear that?"

The faint sound of rotors beating the air grew louder as they listened.

"Helicopters," said Clint. "Get down."

Clint and the others grabbed dirt as what sounded like three choppers passed overhead. When he looked up, he whistled softly. "Those big birds are military issue. Where do you suppose they're headed?"

"Let's find out." Peter launched himself into the treetops, moving swiftly from limb to limb. He disappeared from view within moments, and then quickly returned. "All right," he said, sounding tense and strained, not at all like his usual wisecracking self. "This is the deal: The reason we can't see the mines is because we're at the edge of a cliff here. The mines are directly below. You're only about thirty feet away."

Luke shaded his eyes, peering up at the acrobatic figure in the red-and-blue Spider-Man suit perched in the treetops. "What aren't you telling us?"

"You'd better see for yourselves."

STANDING near the edge of a sharp drop-off, the four Avengers watched as the large military cargo helicopters landed on the ground some one hundred and fifty feet below, their propellers blowing up a thick cloud of powdery dirt.

When the dust cleared, Clint saw three large trucks loaded with crates. Roughly two dozen mutates, mostly men, were unloading the trucks and transferring the crates to the choppers.

Six S.H.I.E.L.D. agents guarded the mutates, their

submachine guns held loosely in their hands. As Clint and the others watched, a heavily furred cat-man stumbled and nearly dropped one of the boxes on the ground. A guard stepped forward and zapped him with a Taser. The cat-man grunted and convulsed on the ground.

"I don't believe it," said Luke, his voice so gruff it almost sounded like a growl. "Tell me that's not *our people* playing slavemasters down there."

There was a high, whining noise, and Clint shouted, "Sniper!" just as a piece of bark exploded near his head. "They're shooting at us. I can't believe it. Even if they don't know that we work for S.H.I.E.L.D., they have to be able to see Cap's uniform."

Clint expected shock from Cap, or a moment of denial. Maybe even an attempt to hail the shooter: *Can't you see we're one of you?* Instead, Steve said, "Barton! Can you tell where the sniper's located?"

"He hasn't hit us yet, so I'm guessing he's shooting from an inclined angle."

"Thanks." Steve sent his shield flying—but the attacker was elusive. In the moment before the shield returned to Steve's hand, a bullet whizzed past.

"We've got to regroup! Take cover!"

They turned and ran.

Peter was closest to the safety of the trees when the huge pteranodon swooped down. He flicked his wrist, sending a jet of web-fluid into the creature's face. It did no good; the creature had Peter in its claws, and its great wings were already beating, lifting them higher into the air.

Steve threw his shield again; it spun out, hitting the pteranodon in the side before returning to Steve's hand. The flying reptile roared, but didn't release Spider-Man.

"Sauron," Luke bellowed. "Let him go!" A bullet pinged off Luke's back, and then another bullet flew past Clint's cheek, barely missing him. He sent three more of his precious remaining arrows winging in the sniper's direction.

Dangling in the air twenty feet above the ground, Peter tried to wrest himself loose of Sauron's grip. "Lykos, I don't want to fight you!"

"Brainchild thought I could feed off you," said Lykos, his claws cutting into Spider-Man's shoulders. "Let's see if he was right." As Clint and the others watched, Sauron opened a beak that looked sharp enough to cut through mastodon bones.

Steve threw his shield again. This time, he hit his target squarely on the right wing, and Sauron dropped to the ground. Peter broke loose, rolling as he hit the dirt.

The Avengers approached Sauron, who was flapping his wings, attempting to fly.

"Stop," said the creature that had been Lykos. "Do not attack." His voice had a raspy, avian quality, like a raven's. The moment he issued the command, Clint found himself unable to move. *It's his eyes,* thought Clint. They were huge; the pupils had turned into spirals, mesmerizing him with their constant, whirling motion.

Sauron shook his long, beaked head—an oddly human gesture from such an inhuman creature. "It's funny. In my village, we all grew up wanting Coca-Cola and Levi's jeans and a hero like Captain America to protect us. It's one of the reasons I first agreed to work with—"

Sauron's last word ended in a strangled croak as the back of his crested skull exploded. Clint felt the spatter of blood and bone and brains on his face as the pteranodon toppled over. "Jesus," said Clint, realizing he could move again. "That shot came from behind us." Either the soldiers from the bottom of the cliff had managed to scale the rock face and maneuver silently around them, or, more likely, they had radioed for reinforcements. As Clint drew his bow, Luke, Peter and Steve moved forward to confront whoever had taken Sauron down.

From the trees opposite them, a dozen tactical S.H.I.E.L.D. guards closed in, their weapons aimed at the Avengers

Steve stepped forward as if the guns were unworthy of his notice. "Soldiers," he said, clipping the end of the word, "this is Captain America. I work for S.H.I.E.L.D. and have a level-eight security clearance." Clint had never heard Cap so furious. "You are acting in direct defiance of S.H.I.E.L.D. protocols. I order you to stand down!"

One of the soldiers, a sunburnt redhead, opened up a sat phone. Clint couldn't make out what he was saying, but assumed he was requesting instructions from a senior officer.

The redheaded soldier seemed to have trouble understanding what the officer on the other end was saying. As Clint watched, he spoke into the phone again, and then listened to the response. When he turned to his fellow soldiers, his face was grim.

Peter looked at Luke. "Did he just say what I think he said?"

Luke cursed eloquently. "Get behind me."

It was the expression on Steve's unmasked face that made Clint finally understand what the others had heard: The S.H.I.E.L.D. agents had been ordered to kill them.

EIGHTEEN

AT first glance, the S.H.I.E.L.D. outpost didn't look like much, just a group of small whitewashed buildings arranged around two rows of palm trees. A hundred feet from the closest building, Natasha, Tony and Jessica waited in the shelter of a makeshift hide composed of dirt, bushes and a few saplings pulled down to form a screen. So far, no one had emerged from any of the buildings.

"Finally," said Tony, as two agents dressed in black bodysuits exited one of the outbuildings and walked toward the largest structure, presumably the location HQ. The two appeared to be chatting companionably. One even laughed.

"No crisis situation here," said Natasha, taking her turn with the binoculars. "In fact, if you block out the jeeps and the military helicopters and the ugly metal Quonset hut, it could be a budget vacation destination."

"You mean the kind where a manic depressive runs

exercises in group humiliation around the swimming pool?" Jessica held out her hand for the binoculars. "Sounds good to me. Throw in a tennis court and a hammock, and I wouldn't mind being stationed here."

Tony lifted the faceplate of his helmet. "You have extremely low standards. Armor, any progress on the Raft file analysis?"

"Negative."

"Not good enough. We need to know more about our friends out there and what they've been hiding. And I mean friends in the ironic, invisible-quotation-marks sense."

"I *know* what you meant," snapped the armor. "I'm programmed with advanced language-inference capabilities. Utilizing them, however, slows the rate at which I crunch numbers."

"Guess he told you," said Jessica.

"Well, even without the computer, we know one thing for sure," said Natasha. "Whatever made them go offline, it wasn't because they were in distress."

"I disagree. We can't be one hundred percent certain yet." Jessica paused to slap at a mosquito. "Maybe there was an attack, and people are injured inside. Or maybe they're sick." The mosquito's whine returned, and Jessica turned and zapped it with an electrical blast from her fingertips. Catching Tony's look, she said, "What? Since you know I've got them, might as well use them."

"I'm assuming we're talking about your powers," said Tony.

"Zap him next," said Natasha.

"Grah." Jessica made a threatening claw shape with

her fingers, and Tony countered with his metal-sheathed hand.

"Okay, that lookout's body language." Natasha pointed to a guard tower that gave its occupant a bird's-eye view of the outpost's perimeter. "He's relaxed, maybe even bored. And look at the bicycle propped there, by that building. Everything is neat and orderly. This place is temporarily short-staffed, but they're not worried." Natasha sat back against the base of a tree and uncapped the canteen. "My guess is that a large number of people have temporarily gone somewhere else for a few hours." She offered the canteen to Tony.

"Hang on a moment." Tony took the canteen. "The mines?" He handed Jessica the water.

"That makes sense," said Jessica. "But we need to take a closer look." She brought the canteen to her lips and tipped her head back. "Tony. You didn't leave me any."

"That would be me," said Natasha.

"You finished all the water?"

"No, I'm the one who should go into the compound. I'm the only one not wearing scarlet and gold. My black jumpsuit will blend in, like on the Helicarrier." Natasha pulled her hair back with one hand. "Can I borrow a ponytail holder? I've noticed most of the female S.H.I.E.L.D. officers wear their hair back."

"This is the only one I've got," said Jessica, removing the elastic from her own hair. "But hang on a moment. How do we know you're not going to stroll in there and tell them where we are?"

"You don't," said Natasha.

She stood up and strode out into the open as if she had every right to do so. She passed a young woman in combat gear and nodded to her, thinking, *I outrank you.* The soldier saluted, and Natasha returned the salute before continuing on to the compound's main structure.

Aware that she was being watched through Jessica's binoculars, Natasha imagined Jessica's frustration when she entered the building. *Guess you'll have to give me the benefit of the doubt, after all.*

The temperature was noticeably cooler inside the main hall, and Natasha enjoyed the blast of air conditioning on the back of her neck. She walked past a taxidermic Tyrannosaurus rex that appeared to have lost a few teeth and a few rows of folding chairs arranged around a small podium. Small flags from all the United Nations' member countries hung at intervals around the room, and the agents Natasha had seen from outside were walking to the back of the room, near the stairs and elevator, where a guard was seated behind a large oak desk. They nodded at him and walked into the elevator.

All right, then, thought Natasha. *My turn.* She approached the guard, thinking, *We've passed each other a dozen times, we barely know each other, but we recognize each other's faces.* It seemed to be working. On the wall behind the guard, there was a framed image of the S.H.I.E.L.D. eagle emblem. Below this was a faded black-and-white picture of Captain

America in a World War II-era leather jacket, standing beside a dapper, suited President Roosevelt; a stout, glum-faced Prime Minister Churchill; and a cheery Stalin, wearing a military cap and greatcoat to go with his stage-villain moustache. Underneath the photograph there was a brass plate engraved with the words of a poem by the Persian poet Saadi that Natasha recognized from the United Nations building in New York City:

> The sons of Adam are limbs of each other
> Having been created of one essence.
> When the calamity of time affects one limb
> The other limbs cannot remain at rest.
> If thou hast no sympathy for the troubles of
> others
> Thou art unworthy to be called by the name of
> a human.

It was all terribly high-minded and inspirational, but Natasha guessed that the young guard sitting in front of the display hadn't bothered to read the poem recently. He had a snub nose and appeared too young to shave, but his small, deep-set blue eyes held a thuggish, stubborn look.

"Wait a moment," he said, just as Natasha was about to walk past him. "Please show your identification."

"I haven't been issued my card yet," said Natasha. "That's why I'm here."

"Where's your temporary card? You can use that

until you get properly processed." There was a touch of irritation in his voice.

This one is just looking for an excuse, thought Natasha.

"Soldier, do you see any insignia on my uniform?"

The guard frowned. "No…"

"That's right. Now, what does that signify?"

Surprised by her belligerent attitude, the guard shook his head. "I'm not sure I understand."

Natasha sighed. "It signifies that I was brought in at level five or higher."

"Oh, right." The guard's face cleared. "You're from the Black Widow program, then? I know your people come in with automatic level five."

"That's right," said Natasha, hoping he hadn't caught the flicker of surprise she had been unable to suppress.

He hadn't. "I'll tell the Lieutenant Commander that you're here." The guard pressed a button on his phone. Looking back at Natasha, he said, "What's the name?"

Chort poderi. She hadn't had time to prepare for this. There would be a list, and her own name would not be on it. Neither would some made-up name. Natasha had to pick someone who had been through the Black Widow program, but was not already known to the guard. "Yelena Belova." It was a gamble, but a small one: Her old friend was not the sort of agent who got sent on the more exotic assignments. "Hang on just a moment, ma'am."

As the guard waited for the person on the other end to pick up the phone, his nostrils flared. Something had given her away. Natasha said, "Thanks," and then moved swiftly toward the exit, as if this were the logical thing to do while waiting to be buzzed upstairs.

"Hey," said the guard. "Where are you going?"

Natasha did not look around. "I forgot something in my room. I'll be right back."

She opened the door and walked calmly outside. The sun was in her eyes as she moved purposefully toward Tony and Jessica. *Come on,* she thought, *tell me you're paying attention.*

Natasha heard the door open behind her, the click of a gun being cocked.

"Halt!"

Natasha stopped and turned slowly. The guard's boyish face was flushed with twitchy excitement. *Wonderful.* Clearly he had been sitting at his desk, bored out of his mind, hoping to shoot someone all day, possibly all week, and now he was finally getting his chance. Assuming Captain America's air of calm authority, Natasha looked back at the guard as if he had temporarily lost his mind.

"Excuse me? Is there a reason you're pointing your gun at a superior officer?"

"I'm pointing my gun at an imposter."

There was a blast of static from the walkie-talkie at the guard's waist, and he picked it up. "Yes, that's right, I'm holding her." He gripped his pistol in two hands, and Natasha could almost hear him praying for her to give him an excuse to shoot.

Then the door opened. A slender blonde woman in a black jumpsuit emerged, and Natasha's heart gave an odd little lurch in her chest as she watched her oldest friend approach as if she were a stranger. Yelena's small gray eyes and long, sharp features gave her a haughty, unfriendly look, and she was usually given cover identities as stern mid-level bureaucrats or austere academics. She was one of those women whose faces were utterly transformed by smiling, but she was not smiling now.

"Yelena," Natasha said. "You're in charge here." It wasn't a question: Part of her had known from the instant the guard had reacted.

"I wondered if you would make it this far," said Yelena. Her face was set and hard. "But of course, you were always exceptional." She said the last word as though it were a particularly vicious slur.

Natasha flipped through her mental playbook of strategies. "If you wanted to lead an operation, you could have just said so." She lifted her eyebrows, inviting a riposte—as if this were a game between friendly rivals, not enemies.

But she had miscalculated. "Do you really think you can hand me an assignment like some cast-off dress?" Yelena's mouth twisted. "You're not the star pupil anymore, Natalia. You betrayed the organization *and* your government. Exceptional doesn't count if you cannot be trusted."

Natasha stared at her oldest friend. "How can you speak to me about trust?"

Yelena gave a harsh laugh. "Please. Don't try to play the wounded doe with me, Natalia. I know you too well."

"And I never knew you at all. What's going on here, Yelena? Why are you working with S.H.I.E.L.D.? Does it have something to do with the Vibranium mines?" Natasha softened her tone. "Of course, it's not safe to leave those kinds of resources lying around, unguarded. If someone doesn't mine it, then sooner or later some terrorist group will take advantage. There are so many tribes and factions in the Savage Land." She paused. "And if the officials who are supposed to be in charge are too blind to see what must be done, a real patriot finds a way to get around them."

"Exactly," said Yelena. "Some of the local clans were already trying to work the mines. If we hadn't moved in when we did, you would have savages armed with a metal that can withstand all kinds of ordnance."

"So you put them to work mining the Vibranium for you, instead."

A nerve beside Yelena's left eye twitched. "I see what you're doing."

"I'm just trying to understand. You always said that we have an obligation to protect the most vulnerable in any society. Surely the Savage Landers are the vulnerable ones here."

"We don't have time for this." Yelena averted her head, breaking eye contact with Natasha. "Guard, take her to the holding cell."

"Yes, ma'am."

The guard moved so that his gun was against Natasha's back.

The sat phone at Yelena's waist flared to life, and she picked it up. "Yes? What? I gave you my orders. I

don't care who he is, I told you to eliminate them."
Yelena dropped her gaze, and Natasha thought, *Clint
and the others. They've found them.*

Natasha threw back her head. "Tony," she yelled at
the top of her voice. "Get to the mines! They're going
to kill Cap and the others!"

Yelena's eyes widened. "You shouldn't have done
that, Natalia." Her eyes glittered with some fierce
emotion. "Guard?"

The boyish guard snapped to attention.

"Shoot her."

The guard smiled as if he had been given a compli-
ment and aimed his gun. In the sky behind him, Natasha saw a red-and-gold blur racing toward her. In
the next moment, Natasha felt a tug as she was yanked
up by the armpits and lifted into the air.

"That went well," said Tony, adjusting his grip on
Natasha so he was supporting her by his left arm.

Tony's helmeted head turned. "Uh, Jessica? You're
not holding on to me!"

"What? No! Aaagh!" Jessica pretended to flail for a
moment, like a cartoon character accidentally walking off a cliff. "Just kidding," she said, giving Tony a
broad grin. "Yeah, I can fly again."

"Think you could have mentioned this earlier,
when we were figuring out who to send where?"

"Sorry," said Jessica, not sounding it.

"And while we're on the subject of bad judgment
calls," said Tony, "you were right, Natasha. Your black
jumpsuit had them completely fooled."

Natasha took a deep breath, fighting the rush of

adrenaline. Her hands still felt like ice, but at least she had her full range of vision back. "I still say it makes no sense to wear costumes that draw attention to you."

"Covert is so yesterday. These days, it's all about branding." Tony adjusted his grip, pulling Natasha closer into his side. A bullet pinged, and then another; he was shielding her, she realized.

"So what's the story with you and that blonde?" Jessica had to shout to be heard over the wind rushing past them. "Know her long?"

"Just for twenty years or so." Which, it turned out, meant not at all. Natasha wondered whether this was an occupational hazard of her profession, or whether it was simply impossible to know anyone well enough to detect the signs of betrayal.

"So you guys went to sexy-assassin school together? How many more of you are...hang on," said Tony. "What's going on, armor?"

"Incoming, mortar bomb detected," said the armor as a blast of heat scorched a trail toward them. "K-6 fin-stabilized—minimum range 660 feet, maximum range 23,750 feet."

"TMI." A sudden rush of air pushed at them. Tony angled his body, changing course. There was a lightning crack of sound, followed by a blast that sent them tumbling backward. Natasha felt the scorching heat of the exploded bomb on her face, followed by a disorienting roll and tumble as Tony fought to right himself.

"Sorry about that," said Tony. "Everyone okay?"

"Well, I'm still here," said Jessica. "But that felt like a quick trip on the world's worst amusement-park ride."

"I think we're out of range now." They were flying much higher than before—the towering trees and volcanic mountains taking on the aspect of a small diorama, a herd of enormous Apatosaurus resembling perfect little toy replicas.

"I think I like the Savage Land better from up here," said Natasha. The left half of her face felt badly sunburned. Maybe there was a reason for wearing masks into battle.

"Agreed," said Tony. "So what exactly are we flying into here?"

"I thought you didn't want too much information," said the armor.

"I was talking to Natasha, armor. Tasha, what did you overhear at the compound?"

A wave of dizziness swept over Natasha, followed by a surge of nausea. "I think some of the S.H.I.E.L.D. troops were questioning the order to kill Captain America...and the others."

"Jessica, grab on to me," said Tony. "Armor, put on some speed here."

"Yes, Mr. Stark. By the way, the Raft analysis is now complete."

"Not now! Just get us to the mines."

There was a tremble in the armor gripping Natasha's waist, and then a rush of wind in her ears as the suit accelerated. Below them, the jungle passed in a blur of brilliant green.

Just when she thought her eardrums would pop, Tony put on the brakes. They hovered in midair, looking down at the tableau below them.

"Oh, my God," said Jessica. Sauron's lifeless body lay sprawled on the ground, his great wingspan making him appear even larger in repose. Around the green-skinned reptile corpse, a dozen S.H.I.E.L.D. troops held Clint, Captain America, Luke and Spider-Man at gunpoint. Clint had an arrow nocked and ready to fire while Steve stood just in front of Luke and Peter, shield held low in his right hand.

"Need a little assistance?" Tony lowered himself until he was hovering directly over his teammates' heads.

"Need a little armor," yelled Peter.

"Got a few spare million in your bank account?" Tony lifted his helmeted head. "Uh-oh. We've got company."

A fraction of a second later, Natasha heard it, too: the distinctive whup-whup sound of a helicopter's rotor blades beating the air, accompanied by the rapid rat-a-tat-tat sound of a machine gun.

Yelena.

"Hell," said Jessica, "they're firing on us." She and Tony swooped around, changing direction to avoid the gunfire. Natasha, who never got motion sickness, felt her stomach flip with the jerky, unpredictable shifts in motion.

Down on the ground, Clint wiped a trickle of blood from his face before aiming his arrow up at their attackers. *The minute he lets that arrow fly,* thought Natasha, *the troops down on the ground will begin shooting.*

"They need backup."

"I know," said Tony, circling round. "I just need to set you down somewhere safe."

"There's no time. I have to jump." She was forty feet or so off the ground. That was survivable, if she did it right. "Neither of you can fight effectively while carrying me."

"But you'll break your neck," said Jessica.

"In the Red Room training facility, we used to do this twice a day before lunch."

Natasha launched herself off Tony's arm, pointed her toes and tucked, trying to recall her gymnastics training. *I need to execute two and a half somersaults and land on my feet with knees bent before rolling.* If she timed it right—and that was a big if—there was a slim chance she might not break anything crucial, like her neck. As an added bonus, she might not get shot if she was rolled up in a tight ball.

It sounded like a reasonable plan, but like most battle plans, it fell apart almost instantly. Natasha had barely completed her first somersault when a bullet winged her back and she hurtled downwards, out of control. Before she had time to blink, she found herself caught in two strong arms: a woman's arms.

"I'm beginning to like you a bit better," she told Jessica as they landed.

"Just evening the score," said Jessica, setting Natasha on her feet. Then one of the S.H.I.E.L.D. ground soldiers fired the first shot, and there was no more time for talk.

NINETEEN

PETER flicked his wrists and sent a jet of his most powerful webbing at the two soldiers to his left, covering their faces. Above him, Jessica and Tony zipped around, firing off blasts at the helicopter, forcing it to land.

I didn't know Jess could fly, he thought, feeling a twinge of envy. *Wish I'd gotten her radioactive spider instead of mine.*

Off to Peter's left, he could hear the crack of gunfire. Natasha had managed to liberate one of the rogue S.H.I.E.L.D. agents' guns and was using Luke's bulletproof body as a buffer while she picked off their opponents. The fighting had kicked up a lot of dust, offering Peter random glimpses of the battle: a grimacing face here, a falling body there, an explosion that split an enormous tree right in half.

Peter whirled, his spider-sense tingling, to find a soldier coming at him, teeth bared, wielding his gun like a club. Peter vaulted over him, netting him with webbing, and then swung him into a knot of three other soldiers. *Four in one blow,* he thought. *Not bad for a city boy.*

Peter looked around and saw that Clint was standing, grim-faced, with blood dripping from a cut above one eye, aiming an arrow at the helicopter's rotor blades. The arrow whistled through the air; to Peter's astonishment, it sheared off an entire propeller blade.

Vibranium. It had to be. The chopper went into a violent spin, and Peter spotted two soldiers bailing out just before the helicopter turned into a massive fireball. One was a woman, a blonde, her hair streaming behind her until her parachute opened.

The dust billowed up into a thick cloud, making it difficult to see or breathe. The rapid gunfire died down to just one or two shots, and Peter heard someone cough.

"Yelena," shouted Natasha, followed by a stream of Russian.

Someone shouted back in the same language, and Peter watched as Natasha aimed her gun. He could just make out the shape of a woman, detaching the deployed parachute from her back. That was the woman from the helicopter, Peter realized, as Natasha zeroed in on her target. *Dear God,* thought Peter, *she's aiming for the woman's head.* Before he had time to react, Captain America's shield came spinning across his field of vision, knocking the weapon out of Natasha's hands as it discharged.

Natasha turned on Steve, furious. "Are you insane?"

"We don't shoot to kill," he shouted back.

There were shouts and curses from the rogue S.H.I.E.L.D. soldiers and a brief volley of return gunfire.

Iron Man flew forward and knocked over two of the shooters while Luke moved in, using his body as a human shield so Clint could reload.

"Cap, I'm out of arrows," said Clint.

"On the bright side, the people firing at us are happily reloading," said Natasha, giving Steve a dirty look.

Peter decided not to mention that his reserves of web fluid were also running low. "Where are the terror chickens when you need them?"

Jessica flew overhead, firing her venom blasts. "So what's the plan, Cap?"

Steve wiped the dirty sweat from his forehead. He looked at each of them in turn, silently taking each team member's measure. Peter felt Steve looking past the Spider-Man mask, with its exaggerated white eyes, and peering into the mess of roiling thoughts racing through his brain. As Steve nodded to him, Peter felt himself go still and calm. Whatever Cap's voodoo was, he could work it without words.

"The plan," Steve said at last, "is to fight them until we win."

Natasha gave a snort of derision. "Don't you mean fight them until we die? If they're shooting to kill us, and we're fighting back to capture them, there's only one way for this to end."

Tony dropped down to stand in front of the other Avengers. "Did someone call for a coffee break? I can't do this on my own, you know. I mean, I probably could, but then you guys would feel even more inferior."

"Not to pander to your ego," Steve said, "but I don't suppose you've got any more tricks up your sleeve?"

"Wow, things must be bad, if you're asking me for help." Tony flipped up his visor. "Armor?"

"Online, Mr. Stark."

"Project twenty-foot radius polar magnetic field."

"I'm afraid there's an insufficient power-cell charge."

Tony sighed. "And what do we do when we don't have enough power?"

"Charging."

The dust had begun to clear. They didn't have much time, thought Peter. "Um, Tony? How long do you think this is going to take?"

Tony spat dust out of his mouth. "Armor, status report."

"Power cells six-point-five percent, Mr. Stark."

Come on, thought Peter, *charge up already.* Now that the dust cloud had settled, he could see the faces of the S.H.I.E.L.D. agents again—some two dozen soldiers, heavily armed. Someone coughed. This was going to be bad, thought Peter.

The blonde, Yelena, stepped forward, looking almost bored, as if she were about to perform a ritual that held no personal meaning for her. "Avengers. Do you surrender?"

Steve stepped forward. "Lady, you are in complete defiance of S.H.I.E.L.D. protocols. I demand that you stand down."

Yelena's smile did not reach her eyes. "You are showing your age, Captain. I am not a lady. You may address me as Lieutenant Commander, or ma'am."

"Sorry, *lady*, but I do not recognize your authority here."

A bullet pinged against Steve's shield; he had raised it just in time. Yelena turned to her left. "Who did that? There will be no shooting until I give the command!"

"She was never good at handling positions of authority," murmured Natasha. "Too strident. Too quick to anger."

"All right," said Yelena. "Since you refuse to surrender, Captain, you leave me no choice but to give the order."

Peter thought about Mary Jane and wondered what she was doing. He couldn't remember what day it was, so he pictured her sitting in her kitchen, drinking coffee, making a to-do list. Buy milk. Pay the credit-card bill. Go to the gym. He pictured the sun shining on her hair, bringing out the lovely dark reds. She would be wearing a T-shirt and boxer shorts, braless, her feet bare, her toenails unpainted.

He wondered how she would take the news of his death, if he wound up dying here. Probably have a good cry with her girlfriends, and then buck herself up with the comforting thought that at least she hadn't married him. I always knew he was going to wind up getting himself killed, she would say. She would meet someone new and get married and get pregnant, and her children would grow up and never even know who he was.

"Team Red," said Yelena in a loud voice. "Eyes on target. Ready to fire. Open fi—"

"Wait!" Natasha stepped past Steve and stood directly in front of Yelena, in the line of fire. "Before you do this, Yelena, I need to ask you a question. Surely you owe me one question before I die?"

Yelena shook her head. "I am disappointed, Natalia. I wouldn't have expected you to be such a coward. Is it really worth it, just to live a few more minutes?"

"I just need to know one thing: Who is in charge of this operation—you, or someone at S.H.I.E.L.D.?"

Yelena gave a contemptuous laugh and said something in Russian.

"She's buying us time," said Clint. "Tony, how're we doing?"

"Come on, armor," muttered Tony. "What have you got?"

"Six point six...six point seven..."

"Divert all other power. How about now?"

"Eight point nine."

"Here," said Jessica. "Try this." She aimed a blast of electricity at the arc reactor in Tony's chest. Tony stumbled back, and then caught himself.

"How about now?" His voice was raspy.

"Eleven."

"I'll take it. Raise the field! But keep the level low. I don't want to pull out anyone's fillings."

"You didn't have to yell," said the armor primly. "Field activated, level low."

"I don't see anything," said Luke. "What kind of a force field did you put up?"

The answer came in a sudden barrage of guns, dog tags, sat phones, glasses, rings and watches, which all flew toward the Avengers as if the pied piper were calling them home. For a moment, all the weapons hung suspended in the air, and then Tony said, "deactivate," and they rained down at the team's feet.

"Sweet Christmas," said Luke.

"And a very happy Chanukah," added Peter.

He watched the shock on their enemies' faces as they realized they had just lost the battle. *Take that, Mary Jane. I'm not dying here, after all.*

TWENTY

THERE was a moment of stunned silence, and then Natasha said, "All right, Yelena. Who organized this operation?" She was dimly aware of Peter, Luke and Jessica moving around her to secure the other troops, but most of her attention was focused on Yelena.

Yelena gave a tight smile. "Oh, here it comes: Natalia Romanova's big scene. Do your friends know why our teachers called you Romanova? Tell me they understand that you are not actually related to the former imperial family." Projecting her voice to reach Steve and the others, she said, "We called your friend here the grand duchess, because she always had to be the center of attention. She didn't have a last name, you see. No mother or father listed."

"This isn't about me, Yelena."

"Of course it's about you. It's always about you. You always needed everyone to tell you again and again how you were the best, the smartest, the strongest, the prettiest. Well, it's my turn to be the Black Widow now. I'm on the inside, and you—you're nothing, a nobody with no family, no friends and no job."

"You didn't beat me out for this assignment, Yelena. I would never have wanted it, and neither would you if you weren't so desperate. You're still second best. Now, tell me, because I know you don't have what it takes to initiate this kind of operation. Whom do you report to?"

"I don't have what it takes?" Yelena's face contorted with rage. "You have no idea." Without warning, Yelena slammed the heel of her hand toward Natasha's chin. Natasha took the blow, and then dabbed the bloody corner of her mouth.

"You've got be kidding. With everything that's going on here, you want to have some kind of grudge match with me?"

"What's the matter? Scared I'll hurt you?" Yelena punched again, but this time Natasha grabbed the other woman's wrist—rotating it and using Yelena's own arm as a lever to propel her into Natasha's knee, and then down on her back.

"Enough of this nonsense. Tell me who's in charge."

Yelena's response was to grab Natasha's elbows and flip her over. "Actually," Yelena said, getting to her feet, "that would be me."

In a blur of motion, Natasha kicked out, scissoring her legs and taking Yelena back down to the ground. "Wrong answer." Natasha grabbed the tight black collar of Yelena's jumpsuit. "Let's try again. Who's running this op?"

Yelena wiped a trickle of blood from her nose. She had always been prone to nosebleeds. "I am."

Natasha moved behind her, still holding the collar. "I doubt that." She twisted her wrist, cutting off Yelena's air. "Ten seconds of this, and you'll black out. A little more, and you won't wake up." Yelena's face began to turn red; she flailed, struggling.

"Natasha!" It was Steve, of course. "Stop it, before you kill her."

Natasha glanced up. "Not if she surrenders. Do you surrender, Yelena?" She relaxed her grip.

It took Yelena a moment before she could speak; when she did, her voice came out in a hoarse croak. "Never."

"All right, then." Natasha leaned in again, and Yelena closed her eyes.

"Natasha! Stop." Steve put his hand on her shoulder. "That's an order!"

"Nat." It was Clint, standing beside her. "You have to let her go."

Natasha looked up. Jessica, Tony, Peter and Luke were all staring at her. She knew without being told that they were giving her one last chance to do the noble thing before they stepped in and forced her to do it. It would be Clint, of course, who would be the enforcer. With a grunt of disgust, Natasha flung herself back off Yelena.

"That is not the way we do things," said Steve, his voice tight with anger.

"I'm beginning to see why your old team fell apart," replied Natasha, getting up. Yelena rolled onto her hands and knees, retching. "What would you like me to do? Offer her a coffee and a call home? Promise her amnesty if she talks? You have no idea what kind of people you're dealing with."

There were bright patches of angry color on Steve's cheeks. "Miss, I cannot tell you how sick and tired I am of hearing that."

Natasha shook her head. "Then you should know there's no room for those kinds of qualms in a situation like this, Captain. If you don't use everything you've got, you're going to let them win." She heard a gasp from behind her and whirled. Yelena was sitting back on her heels, her eyes wide as she looked up at the sky.

Then Natasha heard the leathery flap of enormous wings, accompanied by a hoarse, hawkish scream. She looked up and nearly screamed herself when she saw Sauron swooping down at her with bared claws. But she was not his target. Sauron snatched Yelena by the front of her uniform, the back of his crested head dripping gore. His huge wings beat the air slowly as he attempted to gain altitude.

Natasha stared up at the sky, shielding her eyes from the sun. "How is he still alive, Clint?" Too late, she remembered that they weren't on speaking terms.

"He must have some kind of healing factor, like Wolverine."

"Wait a minute, guys," said Peter. "I'm getting a bad tingle here."

"Mr. Stark," said the armor, "I am detecting a level-white energy flux."

"Oh, man, that's not good. Raise the repulsor shield!"

"Shield vector can only protect a three-foot radius, Mr. Stark."

Luke turned to Peter. "What's a level-white energy flux?"

"Trust me," said Peter, "you don't want to know."

"Everybody, get close to me—now!" Tony raised his arms, and a white light burst from the palms of his metallic gauntlets. Clint grabbed Natasha, pulling her back with him as the energy pouring out of Tony's palms formed a dome around the seven Avengers.

Through the scrim of the protective energy shield, Natasha could make out Sauron's reptilian form carrying Yelena off like a monster out of some old horror movie. Suddenly, the sky behind them turned dark. A fierce wind whipped through the trees, nearly bending them in half. Sauron's great wings rippled; he threw back his head and opened his beak as if to scream, but no sound emerged.

Inside the dome, Natasha felt the air pressure change and closed her eyes. Through her eyelids, she saw a flash of brilliant white, followed by a deep rumble of sound that vibrated through her very bones. The ground trembled underfoot as the explosion ripped through the jungle, and Natasha lost her balance. The deep groaning vibration continued; Natasha felt a sharp pain in her sinuses, as if she were descending too quickly in an airplane. She stumbled into someone who drew her in, cupping the back of her head in his hand as he held her against his chest.

Clint. She breathed in the distinctive smell of him mingled with the salt of sweat and thought, *This is dangerous.* Yet she could not make herself move away.

Then the pressure lifted, and Natasha opened her eyes. Clint released her. "They're gone. Vanished."

At first, Natasha didn't understand. "Who?"

"Everyone who wasn't standing right next to us." His tone was clinical, detached. It was as if she had imagined him holding her a moment earlier.

Luke scanned a bloody patch on the ground "Is that all that's left of Sauron and Yelena?"

"All those soldiers I tied up." Peter sounded dazed. "Oh, God."

"Not your fault," said Steve. "You didn't drop that bomb."

Natasha spotted a few strands of golden hair caught between two rocks. She crouched down to pick them up. *Yelena.* All those talks about teachers and boys. The time they had swiped a bottle of vodka from the teachers' lounge and tasted the burn of alcohol for the first time. Experimenting with makeup together, learning how to dismantle and reassemble a Makarov pistol, testing their skills with explosives, practicing their dance moves to Mumiy Troll and Zemfira.

It had all been a lie. One more lie in a life built of lies. Natasha brushed her old friend's hair off her palms.

"I'm sorry your friend died like that," said Clint.

Natasha stood up and felt a dizzying head rush that made the day go dark again for a moment. "I'm not."

"Don't hold a wake just yet," said Tony. "Armor,

did anyone survive the explosion who wasn't in the dome?"

"I am detecting two life-forms retreating—one human, one mutant. Both are badly burned, but not deceased."

"How is that even possible?" Luke stared at the circle of scorched earth where the bomb had detonated. There was almost no trace of the two dozen soldiers who had been there a few moments earlier, and the smell of burnt wood and fabric mingled with the unnerving odor of charred flesh. "I don't know about you, Cap, but I don't think even my thick hide could withstand that kind of a blast."

"Sauron mentioned something about the Weapon X program," said Natasha. "Could they have ramped up his healing ability to the point where he could survive something like this?"

Propping his leg up on a small boulder, Clint used his utility knife to cut a strap from his vest. "I guess it's possible. Could your friend have received some treatments, as well?" He wrapped the strap around his ankle, which looked swollen.

"Yes, maybe." She watched him sheathe his knife again. "Is your ankle broken, or just sprained?"

"Sprained, I think."

"Feel up to going after them?"

"We can't," said Jessica, looking up at the sky. "We have bigger problems to deal with first."

The small, dark shape in the sky grew steadily larger as it descended, revealing itself at last as the distinctive blimp-bottomed, flat-topped S.H.I.E.L.D. Helicarrier.

"You wanted answers, Miss Romanova," said Steve. "It appears we're about to get them."

Natasha looked out at the treeline, weighing her options.

"Don't do it," Clint said. "You're a part of this now."

She glanced up at him. "I don't think Cap here agrees with that."

Steve nodded his head in acknowledgment. "I won't deny that you've been a valuable asset, but you crossed a line back there. We don't torture answers out of people."

"I understand." *You're nothing—a nobody with no family, no friends and no job.*

"Do I get a vote?"

Natasha looked at Jessica in surprise.

"When you told her to stop," said Jessica, "she stopped. She argued with you, but she stopped."

Tony lifted the visor of his helmet. "Do I get a vote? Yes, of course I do—money always gets a vote. So here's my take: We came together at the Raft breakout by chance or fate or whatever the hell it was. And then you came up with the idea of making us a team again. It was a good idea, because the bad guys are working together—which means we need to work together, too. They've got mad scientists and shape-shifting super-fighters and high-tech experimental weapons and God knows what else. So we need all the help we can get.

"I watched Red here stroll into a top-security S.H.I.E.L.D. outpost and stroll right out again. She got caught because of Blondie back there, but you know what she did then? She risked her neck to warn us that you guys needed help."

"I didn't know that," said Steve. "How does everyone else feel?"

"I think she should be given the choice to stay." Clint's face was impassive, unreadable. Natasha was ready to swear he wasn't angry with her any longer. Still, something had changed. She just didn't know what.

"How about you, Peter?"

"Personally, I don't think I can comment. I'm an outsider here."

"You don't have to be," said Steve.

"It's not you guys, it's me. Let's just say I've got commitment issues."

"Too bad," said Luke. "My take? I say, the girl is badass. We need some of that."

"I'm sorry, but I can't agree to this." Steve looked up at the Helicarrier, which was now only twenty feet from the ground, its propellers stirring up the dust. He turned back to face Tony and the others. "You can't be an Avenger and have no moral code."

"The real question is, can you have a moral code and still work with S.H.I.E.L.D.?" There was no trace of Tony's usual sarcastic tone. "Because according to them, Lykos has been dead for more than a year."

Steve stared at him, not comprehending. "What?"

"I finally unlocked the Raft files. Out of the forty-two escaped inmates, fourteen are listed dead by S.H.I.E.L.D.—including Jerome Beecham, Nekra Sinclair and Karl Lykos."

"I don't understand," said Jessica. "Why does S.H.I.E.L.D. think they're dead? Some kind of a clerical error?"

Tony shook his head. "If it were an error, the files wouldn't have been locked."

"No wonder Maria Hill seemed so upset about our re-forming the Avengers." Steve stared up at the Helicarrier. "She needed our help to recapture the Raft prisoners, but she had to lock up the files."

"Or else we'd see that the folks we're chasing are supposed to be dead," said Luke.

"So these guys weren't just stockpiling Vibranium," said Steve. "They were stockpiling super-powered criminals."

"And from what Lykos was saying, it sounds as though they were experimenting on them," said Peter. "But who are we talking about? Is this a rogue S.H.I.E.L.D. op?"

"Or does this trace back to the Black Widow program?" Jessica pulled back her hair, tucking it behind her ears. "This doesn't seem like something S.H.I.E.L.D. would do."

"Let's not rule out the possibility of some other group…Hydra, perhaps." Natasha pulled her hair out of its ponytail. "Here's your hair tie back."

"You're right. It could be Hydra. I hadn't thought of that."

"Problem is, it's all conjecture. We don't know who they are," said Tony. "But they sure as shiitake know who we are."

"This is bad," said Luke. "This is the kind of bad

that makes me want to stay home with the nice garden-variety muggers and addicts and gangs. I say we go big on this. Talk to Anderson Cooper. Make a stink."

Peter shook his head. "We do that, the bad guys go to ground. Disappear. Re-form in some new shape. We can't trust anyone with this."

"Yes, we can," said Steve. "We can trust one another."

Shielding their eyes from the wind and dust, the New Avengers stood and watched in silence as the Helicarrier landed in the field in front of them. A door opened, and a staircase stretched out until it reached the ground. The slim, uniformed figure of Maria Hill emerged, flanked by two guards.

"Captain," she said as she approached him. "Mr. Stark. We're so pleased to see that you are unharmed."

"Yeah, we're unharmed," said Steve. "No thanks to you. Do you have any idea how many people you just killed here? Did you decide that we would just be collateral damage—or were you actively trying to murder us, too?"

The S.H.I.E.L.D. guards cocked their rifles.

Maria raised one hand. "Stand down, soldiers. Captain Rogers, the drone was preprogrammed an hour ago, and we had no idea that you were here. You have not kept us apprised of your whereabouts. If you had been in communication with us, we would never have ordered the drone attack. You are all valuable assets. I assure you, we had no intention of harming you."

"That's nice to hear," said Natasha. "Do you think you can explain the *nature* of the mission?"

"Ms. Romanova," said Maria, narrowing her eyes. "I did not realize that you were involved in this operation. The last I heard, you had escaped S.H.I.E.L.D. custody along with the other Raft criminals. Perhaps *you* can explain *your* presence here? Or should I just assume that you were working with your colleague Yelena Belova?"

"She came here because she was investigating the escaped Raft prisoners, ma'am," said Clint. "Same as us."

"I see. You are aware, Agent Barton, that Ms. Romanova attended a school whose sole purpose was to train her to seduce the gullible?"

"I was raised in a circus, ma'am. We lose our gullible early."

Maria shook her head. "Unbelievable. I think we need to take Agent Romanova in for questioning." She gave Clint a hard look. "This time, I will take charge of the prisoner myself." She motioned to her guards. "Take her into custody."

The guards stepped forward, and Clint moved to block them. "I wouldn't do that if I were you."

"Agent Barton, step away from the prisoner."

"With respect, ma'am, I answer to Captain America."

"Captain Rogers, please tell your man to step away from my prisoner."

Natasha felt her mind snap into battle alertness.

Steve moved so his shield blocked both of them from the guards. "You can't have her."

"Excuse me?"

"You heard me. She stays with us."

"I'm afraid that my authority supersedes yours in this."

"You want to take this to Washington? Fine by me. I'll tell the president how you nearly killed us," said Steve. "Or do you really expect us to believe that you just set a timer on your drone and left it on auto-pilot?"

Maria's brows came together. "Are you calling me a liar?"

The note of outrage sounded genuine to Natasha. So either Maria Hill was telling the truth, or she was a world-class liar—better, perhaps, than Natasha herself.

"*You* might have contacted *me*," said Tony. "After all, the Avengers don't cause civilian casualties. Drones do."

"Ah, the Avengers." Maria gave them a tight smile. "Forgive me. I wasn't aware you had re-formed the team. Am I to understand that the Black Widow is part of this enterprise?"

"Yes," said Steve, without equivocation or embellishment.

He's decided to vote yes on me, thought Natasha, *and he's the kind of person who will stand by his decision. From here on in, in his eyes, I'm an Avenger.* Natasha was dumbfounded. Didn't he realize how easily she could betray their trust?

It's a good thing I am on the team. They have no more sense of self-preservation than a bunch of preschoolers.

"Well," said Maria. "It seems you have seduced the whole group. I, however, believe you still pose a security risk. So, Captain America, what's it going to be? Do you release Agent Romanova to my custody, or do we have to resolve this some other way?"

Tony looked at Jessica. "Did she just threaten us?"

"Oh, man," said Luke. "This day just won't end."

"It'll end," said Peter. "It just doesn't look like it's going to end well."

There was buzz from the sat phone at Maria's waist. "Excuse me." She picked up the phone. "Yes?" Suddenly her whole body tensed. "Yes, sir. Standing by, sir." Her eyes flicked over to Jessica, and then up, to a one-man jet that appeared over the horizon. Blunt-nosed and impossibly small, the plane was also impressively fast. Within moments, it landed squarely in front of Maria.

The top popped up, revealing Nick Fury's scowling, eyepatched face.

"Director," said Maria, a little stiffly. "It's good to see you."

"Wish I could say the same." Fury uncurled himself from the tiny cockpit. "I'm going to need a full report on everything that went down from the Raft breakout through today. I have to say, I am not pleased that you have allowed a rogue S.H.I.E.L.D. operation to get this far. How did they manage to fly under your radar for so long? Then, when you do decide to act, you act so precipitously that you manage to lose Karl Lykos and Yelena Belova."

"But…"

"We'll continue this in private." Fury turned to Jessica. "As for you, Special Agent Drew, you've done well. We located the Hydra mole, so you may consider that assignment completed."

Jessica's face broke out in a delighted grin. "Yes, sir. And after my debriefing, will you be filling me in on the disposition of the Hydra agents I've been working with?"

Fury gave her a slightly ironic look of surprise. "Absolutely not."

As Jessica made a little moue of disappointed surprise, Fury moved on to Natasha. "Agent Romanova, the Black Widow. I've heard a rumor that you're working with S.H.I.E.L.D. now. Is that true?"

"Not with S.H.I.E.L.D., Director Fury. With the New Avengers."

Fury's eyebrows lifted. "I see. Well, then, you're not under my jurisdiction." He looked at Tony and Steve in turn. "Stop by and talk with me when you have a chance. Seems we all have some catching up to do."

Maria's mouth thinned. "But, Director..."

Fury held up a hand. "Not now. Cap, do you and your team need a ride back to New York?"

"Thanks, but we've got our own plane," said Tony.

"Suit yourselves," said Fury, heading toward the Helicarrier. Hill followed him reluctantly, casting a dark glance back at the assembled heroes.

The great ship's engines started up, startling a flock of brilliantly plumed Archaeopteryx from the tops of the trees. Clint followed their flight with his sharp archer's eyes, gauging distances and angles of release.

"If I had any arrows left, that could have been lunch."

"Or dinner," said Jessica. "What time is it, anyway?"

"Here or back home?"

"Home."

"It's six o'clock in the evening here," said Tony. "Back in New York, it's still six in the morning."

"Come on," said Steve. "Time to head out, before something else attacks us." A dinosaur trumpeted in the distance, as if in agreement.

For a moment, Natasha felt the familiar, inchoate sadness that always hit her at the end of a mission. Another identity discarded, another mask removed, revealing the blankness beneath. Then she reminded herself that this time was different. She wasn't abandoning a persona, she was inventing one.

"So," said Jessica, falling into step beside her. "You got a place to stay, back in Manhattan? 'Cause now that I'm not an active S.H.I.E.L.D. agent, I'm going to need to find my own apartment."

"You want to become roommates?"

"Sure. Why not?"

"Are you messy, or neat?"

"A complete slob. You?"

"Neat freak."

They smiled at each other. It was, Natasha thought, just like the beginning of a movie. Or maybe it was like real life. Either way, she was looking forward to whatever came next.

EPILOGUE

CLINT stood outside the Brooklyn brownstone and double-checked the address on his phone. It was a nice block, lined with other brownstones and small trees, but the neighborhood hadn't been completely gentrified, meaning there were more pawn shops and pizza joints than big-name outlets and banks. Clint shifted the package he was carrying into his other hand so he could ring the doorbell. He felt first-date nervous, wondering whether the black T-shirt and jacket were appropriate for the occasion, worried that he had spent too much on his present, or not enough. On the whole, he thought he'd rather be back in the Savage Land, fighting something with too many teeth.

There was a click as someone looked through the keyhole, and then a series of clicks as locks were undone. "Hey," said Luke. "You made it."

Not sure how to respond to this, Clint shoved his package at Luke as he walked in the door. "Here."

"Thanks." Luke was dressed in a T-shirt that said "Big Daddy" in bright-orange letters. Clint suddenly felt overdressed.

"Nice shirt."

"Blame Tony for that." Luke looked down at himself. "The man's a billionaire, and all he got me is this lousy T-shirt."

"As I told you, I'm experiencing a little money-flow problem at the moment," said Tony, emerging from a back room with a bottle of root beer in his hand. Tony was wearing a polo shirt and dark gray chinos the same shade as the shadows under his eyes.

"I don't see how it's even possible for you to have money problems." Peter came up to shake Clint's hand and clasp his shoulder. The bruises on his face had faded to faint yellow smudges.

"Still on the fence about joining the team?"

"Afraid so. But I was glad to get the invitation." Peter lowered his voice. "You see Natasha since we got back?"

"Only when we all met up at Tony's penthouse."

"Ah."

For some reason, Clint felt he had to explain himself. "I don't date people I work with. Now that we're both officially Avengers, it's just—it's too messy. Too complicated."

"True. And of course, she's living with Jessica. That might be awkward."

Clint frowned, thoroughly baffled, and then tried to cover it up. "Uh…yeah." He didn't want to drag this conversation out by asking questions.

Peter laughed. "Man, you're more clueless about women than I am."

Clint walked into a room filled with framed prints of old movie posters from the fifties, sixties and seventies, including *Planet of the Apes*. There was a record player, and the soulful sound of Al Green singing "Tired of Being Alone" filled the room with its up-beat lament. "Hey, Clint," said Steve, scooping up some spinach dip with a nacho. "That was a good training session last night. Whoops," he said, as a glob of the creamy dip fell onto his tie.

"Here," said Jessica. "I've got it." She dabbed at the stain, looking very pretty in a gray knit dress. "Did you get a chance to read the report I sent you, Clint?"

"I skimmed it."

"Clint, you can't just glance at a thirty-page document that Natasha and I have been compiling for weeks. Do you realize how many leads we have to sift through to decide which ones to pursue?" She raked her hair back from her face. "We've done all the research on Lykos and Yelena's whereabouts. The least you could do is assist with the analysis."

"By the way," said Steve, "Tony, Luke and I just got some good intel on a few of the other escaped convicts."

Clint gave him a look. "Suckup."

Jessica rounded on him. "Hey, at least he's doing his part! You're not even reading."

"I do my thinking on my feet. You know I'm no good with paperwork, Jess."

"This isn't an expense report! Did you at least read the section where I did an analysis on whether or not

Maria Hill could have recaptured them, if she wanted to?" Jessica's eyes widened. "Oh, my God. You didn't even read that?"

"No, I did. I mean, I'm pretty sure I read that part."

"What did it say?" She folded her arms over her chest.

Clint stuffed a chip in his mouth. "That, um, Maria Hill might have recaptured Lykos and Yelena. If she wanted to."

"Hey, what did I say about shop talk?" Jessica Jones, Luke's wife, emerged from a back room carrying a pink blanket on her shoulder. Clint assumed there was a baby underneath, but he couldn't see any of it.

"Hawkeye brought this for Danielle," said Luke, unwrapping the brightly colored red-and-yellow paper.

"I, uh, wasn't completely sure what to get."

"I'm sure it's—huh." Luke held up the box, which said "The Invisible Woman" in bright-red letters. "It's, uh, is this a Fantastic Four thing?"

"No, it's an anatomically correct model," said Clint, turning the box so the clear-plastic side was up, revealing the contents. "See, you can put it together, all the organs and everything, and then the skin is transparent."

"It's great," said Jessica Jones brightly.

"Obviously, she won't be able to play with it right away, but I figured you'd get so many stuffed animals and booties and things…" Clint's voice trailed off as he caught sight of Natasha, coming out of the kitchen carrying a huge tray of lasagna. She was wearing jeans and a loose, dark-green sweater that fell off one shoulder. "Anyway, I can always return it if it's not the right thing."

"No, it's a great gift," said Jessica. "I'm sure Danielle will love it when she's a little older. I'll put it next to the frog-dissecting kit."

Clint suddenly felt his gift was not inappropriate at all. "A dissection kit? Who would buy a baby something like that?"

"Who do you think?" said Luke, but Clint was already making his way toward Natasha, who was carving up the lasagna with a sharp knife.

"Hi, there, stranger," said Natasha.

"Hey."

This was the first time they'd spent any time together that hadn't been taken up with war-room strategizing, and Clint felt pretty sure he owed Natasha some kind of apology or explanation. He'd done his best to put her out of his mind, because what he had told Peter was true: He didn't date co-workers. Once you started sleeping with a woman you saw all the time, the woman started to expect things. She figured you should remember her birthday, the day you met, the name of her favorite childhood friend. Clint didn't work that way. He couldn't even remember his own birthday, for crying out loud. He wasn't any good at relationships, the kind normal people had.

"Listen, Natasha…"

She paused, the lasagna knife in her hand. "I want to ask you something." She looked up at him, her eyes startlingly green, and Clint realized he'd been lying to himself. He hadn't been staying away from Natasha because of what she might expect from him. He'd been scared of what he might want from her.

"Ask me anything," he said.

"I want you to teach me how to throw a knife."

For a moment, he was caught off guard and couldn't think how to respond. He recovered quickly, though. "Yeah. Sure. Why not?"

"I've had lessons, of course, but my aim when the target is moving is not as precise as I'd like."

"I'll work with you."

"I want to learn axes, too."

"I've got some of those back at my place." He tried not to think what else might happen, with the two of them practicing what circus folk called the impalement arts. There was no hint of flirtation in her manner, so it was probably best not to get his hopes up.

"Next Sunday at 3 p.m.?"

"It's a date," said Clint, and then felt a wave of embarrassment. *It's a date.* Could he be any more obvious? "Excuse me. I need to get a drink." He aimed himself at the side table with the sodas.

"Careful," said Jessica Jones, pouring herself a ginger ale. "Sounds to me like you're about to give away your only advantage."

In the background, Al Green had stopped complaining he was tired of being alone and begun a new song, suggesting they stay together.

"All right, guys," said Tony, setting a camera on the table. "Avengers assemble!"

"Come on, Hawkeye," said Luke's wife, taking Clint by the hand. "You'll figure it out eventually."

The others crowded around, smiling for the camera. Out of the corner of his eye, Clint saw the pink blanket folded back to reveal the baby's face. She wasn't as bad-looking as some babies, he supposed. Not completely scrunched up, at least. And then she looked up at him and smiled.

The camera caught him looking down with a bemused expression on his face. Natasha appeared to be saying something that made Peter and Jessica crack up, while Tony and Steve stood arm in arm, like old Army buddies. At the center of it all, Luke and his wife exchanged conspiratorial glances, as if they knew more about what was going on behind them than they were letting on.

For a team of orphans and outcasts with no place else to go, it was as good as a family portrait.

END